In Private Life

In Private Life

BARBARA HOLLAND

THE AKADINE PRESS

1997

To my family

In Private Life

Part One

CHAPTER ONE

*I*t was that time of year when I really need a general anesthetic. The time of year when my husband says, "Is that all the scotch we have left? I thought there was another whole bottle."

The time of year when the school day seems to keep shrinking, and the space around it expanding. When it takes forty minutes to find all the children's boots and mittens, and get them on, and the children go out to play and before the echo of the closing door has faded they come back, and circle around and around the kitchen complaining aimlessly and tracking mud.

It was the evening of January 29, always an ugly date no matter how you look at it. The phone rang.

"Hi, babe," it said breezily. "This is Bill Emery. Remember me?"

Who ever forgets? The housewife's heart is a locket full of bits of hair. Names. Bill Emery: not the most important name, but the first. A man who, on the other end of the phone, could see me, on my end, as exactly fifteen years old, in red lipstick and rolled-up jeans, transparently grateful for love.

"I got your phone number from your folks. I'm on my way to St. Thomas, and I wondered if I could abduct you and take you along."

On the couch my husband was snoring gently, his book, still held sternly upright in both hands, rising and falling with the murmurous sound. Outside, the snow had been on the ground, the same snow, for five solid weeks, and I could no longer remember what was underneath it. Except, of course, for the things that pretty much had to be under it, like the snow shovel and my other glove.

Bill hadn't said anything about guarding my image like a precious candle flame through all the years, but I took that for granted, and he could tell me about it later, on the beach.

"It'll take me ten minutes to pack," I said. "Where shall I meet you?"

He laughed at my ready wit. He was, he said, between planes, and sorry he didn't have time to come out and see me, and meet my husband, but he called to say hello anyway.

"Hello," I said sourly.

All dreams come true, and in the process turn out to have been a joke all along.

Of course, there isn't any basic, scientific reason why our old loves shouldn't call us up, one of these winter days, and invite us to run off to a tropical isle with them. Heaven knows I think enough about calling *them* up, and sometimes even look up their phone numbers in out-

of-town directories, but I never actually call. I'm embarrassed. I'd have to say, "Remember me? I used to be—"
and give my maiden name. If I can still remember it.

It seems so long ago.

I am a housewife.

Sometimes a person arrives at this condition suddenly;
open a door and walk in and there it is; sometimes it
sneaks up on you in a series of little creeps and rushes,
and then drops over you like a wet towel from on high,
one day while you're squatting down picking bubble gum
out of the bathroom rug. You look up and think, "Hey,
how did I get *here*, of all places?"

It's only slightly consoling to think that everyone else
is here too. It still seems like a funny place to be. Nobody
ever said, when I was fifteen and thought I was Joan of
Arc, and Bill Emery thought I made the sun come up in
the morning, that this was where I was going, in stops
and starts and roundabout ways, but inexorably going,
straight to this bathroom rug, this bubble gum.

I think of all of us, all those pretty girls in high school
with me, with their red mouths and careful hair and their
books carried slung against their hips, moving along the
various paths to converge on the same bubble gum and the
same pantry shelves (baked beans and hot dogs? corned
beef hash and eggs?). How scattered and different the boys
must be now, while all the girls, right this minute, whatever other jobs they may hold or other titles they may use,
have simultaneously given up using their fingernails on the
gum and gone to get the lawn mower's can of gasoline.

Like some kind of compulsory dance. A chorus line. A

million housewives moving in perfect unison, carrying the cereal bowls from the breakfast table to the sink.

I wish people would stop telling their girl children about options. Options, forsooth. What they can opt is either straight housewifery, with at least their late evenings free to read, or housewifery and an outside job, with their late evenings free to fold the laundry.

You can go to law school or not go to law school, but either way you have to feed and change the baby and scrape the cold fried egg off the breakfast plates and fish the socks out from under the couch.

There is no escape.

Some people, who must lead oddly sheltered lives, think I mop the kitchen floor because I am frightened of my husband, or undereducated, or brainwashed. I don't. I mop it because somebody has to. If somebody doesn't, it gets unwholesome and your feet stick to it. Some of the stuff that was spilled turns black, and some of it grows fur. Mop it, or boil it down for soup.

Somebody has to call the plumber, and see the cats are fed, and wash the frying pan.

A housewife is a person who does things that have to be done by her. A man is a person who does things that, in the rare cases where they have to be done at all, like collecting the garbage, don't have to be done by *him;* someone else could do them instead. When he gets flu, someone else does.

Sometimes you can get a man to help you around the house, but remember the operative word is "help." It is your job, and he's helping you. No matter how long and diligently he may perform his allotted tasks, neither of you will ever forget that this is strictly voluntary labor. Charity. He does not abandon his amateur status, and he doesn't have to do anything well, either. If he doesn't happen to feel like it, or he's tired or mad at you or wants to watch the World Series, you can have it back. It was yours to start with. And you'll do it. Somebody must.

My husband rather likes to cook, and sometimes volunteers to make dinner for weeks and weeks at a time. Then he gets sick of it. For three nights running he can't think of anything to have but bacon and eggs, and then he turns it back over to me.

Well, *somebody* has to get dinner. I don't see any way out of it, and believe me, I've looked. I really can't eat frozen pizza every night, and who can afford McDonald's seven times a week, which would very likely give us scurvy anyway?

A long time ago, under another name, I loved to cook. It's hard to remember. I have a lovely recipe for linguine with artichokes, and one for an apple cake, but I can scarcely bear to make them now, even if the children would eat artichokes. I hate cooking. I hate the horrible, haunting, inescapable alwaysness of dinner. In the mornings, I feel swell. By two in the afternoon I notice an itchy uneasiness in the back of my head, as if something is following me. By four its cause becomes apparent. I go and stare into the freezer in numb despair, and then I go and look on the shelves, and then I begin to think about just getting in the car and driving somewhere. Anywhere.

Casseroles. Torn-out recipes from women's magazines

and Sunday papers. Hopeful scraps of them all over the house. Exciting ways to add glamor to ordinary meals by dousing them with canned mushroom soup. Powdered onion soup. Top with swirls of shaving cream for appe-teasing eye-appeal. Ten Taste-tempting Ideas for Leftover Dinosaur. Leftover dog. Boil the one that tips over trash cans, a stick-to-the-ribs treat for those hearty winter ap-petites. For a family-pleasing novelty, serve it in the trash can. Apple in mouth. Dead sneaker in mouth.

Nasty little pre-breaded frozen things, cold and limp. Instant goldfish.

Stuff suspended in Jell-O.

All those combinations of soup and tuna.

Canned baked beans, bland and doughy.

Black depression: I run my finger along the shelf, my stomach tense with loathing.

Sardines? Sardines and beans? Sardines and apple-sauce?

Spaghetti?

We had spaghetti last night. I had leftover spaghetti for lunch.

Something on rice, maybe. Creamed hash on rice? Creamed sardines? Creamed beans?

There are signs of a mouse. The rice bag has been nib-bled. Why doesn't one of our overweight cats do some-thing about it?

Creamed cat.

Canned tomatoes, elbow macaroni, water chestnuts, brown sugar, a jelly glass containing two petrified paint-brushes and still smelling faintly of turpentine; mace, coriander, turmeric, napkins, chicken broth, and a mysterious splotchy-looking paper bag they needn't think I'm going to open.

I could get in the car and just start driving.

Actually, the whole family hates dinner. You'd think there'd be some way of dodging something we all dread, but I haven't found it yet.

Sometimes I think I wouldn't mind it so much if I were allowed to eat it somewhere else. In the garage, maybe.

Emily sits on the edge of her chair, eats swiftly and is gone, as if a sudden draft had sucked her up the stairs. Ben goes into a trance and eats automatically, anything within reach; I have to snatch away his napkin. Matthew's health is stricken, nightly. He turns white, and droops and sighs, and toys with his fork. He survives entirely on contraband refined sugar, in a nutritional vacuum like a laboratory rat. My husband, who was brought up to believe it the height of rudeness to say anything at all at the table, regardless of provocation, sits staring into his plate in speechless horror and dismay, as if I had served him his own foot.

But every night I make something and put it on the table, and call the children to wash their hands. There seems to be no available option there at all.

Almost the only option I can think of, offhand, is not having children. This is a newly popular one, and a lot of women are using it, and feeling offensively virtuous about it, too, and a lot of women who didn't use it are sorry they didn't. Seventy per cent, or ninety per cent, or whatever, depending on which survey you read, of all parents, if they had it to do over again wouldn't. It's chic to hate kids now. They're expensive and ungrateful and they use up natural resources. Babies are okay only for remote tribes in places like Borneo, where they mostly eat caterpillars and don't drive cars. I suppose there's some point in this, even if it does mean that in a couple of generations, or non-generations, everyone will be caterpillar-eaters and there won't be any more civilization. Since I tend to think, fuzzily, of civilization as Bach and the Elgin Marbles rather than petroleum, it seems kind of a shame. Besides, after a while the remote tribes will get around to inventing cars, and strip-mining, and Baggies, and we're back where we started.

Guiltily, I rather like kids. Even my own aren't really so dreadful. They keep my slang up to date.

They keep you limber. Childless people expect things to stay clean, and go as planned, and planes to depart on time. When they don't, childless people are shattered. Parents, on the other hand, expect anything and everything to happen, and know deep in their bones that the night before they're leaving for vacation two out of any three given children will get chicken pox.

For another thing, I've always been dubious about the afterlife. It's hard to believe that even thus translated I would be able to play a harp on a cloud, or off either, but I do like to think that my kids will be trampling around on solid ground when I'm under it. There must be something blunt and sudden about the endings of the childless.

Kids fasten you to the past, too. You tell them things. They even want to hear things, and certainly no one else you know is going to sit still for your childhood reminiscences.

At breakfast, Matt and Ben say, "Tell about when you found the lifeboat, in Florida."

"It was a long time ago," I say, pushing down the toaster. "It was early in the morning."

"How old were you?" asks Matt, who knows perfectly well, but it goes with the story.

"I was ten. My brother was with me. He was five. We were walking down the beach, very early, before breakfast."

And it all rises up in front of me: the glittery pale light over the sea where the sun was coming up through a drift of cloud, and the beach empty except for the scallops of seaweed left by the tide, and two children walking beside the thump and hiss of small waves, scuffing canals in the damp sand with their toes. I see it, and maybe they see it too. Maybe my memories will somehow reprint themselves in my children, and become their memories. An immortality positively dizzying to think about.

When my grandmother was a young girl in Colorado, a long time ago, she went to a dance one winter night. It was cold. She went in a sleigh, with friends. Her young man had given her a flower; I don't know what kind of flower, or where he got it in the winter, but I think of it as a small, plain, red rose. She wore it pinned on her coat. When she got to the dance and came inside the warm house and took off her coat, the flower fell apart. Broke like thin glass. From the dry cold, I suppose, and then the warmth.

She remembered this when she was an old lady, and told me about it, and I remembered it and told my daughter.

I hope Emily remembers. I hope, when she has daughters of her own, she will tell them about their great-great-grandmother's rose, and how the sleigh-runners creaked in the dark, and then the lights and voices inside, and the sudden small scatter of red petals breaking onto the floor. It will have been almost a hundred years ago by then.

That flower seems almost reason enough to have children. If I had it to do over again, I would, and take my place in the generations, slung between the past and the future and fastened tidily at both ends, like a hammock.

Children are a nuisance, of course. On crowded buses they ask you how the sperm gets from the penis to the egg, and why is that lady so ugly? They have nightmares, tantrums, and toys that come apart into literally thousands of little pieces that keep turning up behind the couch cushions and under even the wariest foot. They bring home strange diseases and are sick for two days and give them to you and you're sick for a month. Since television, they've lost some of the ability to amuse themselves, and tend to hang around and whine. They get peanut butter all over everything. They are always *there*. They do not disappear after the first act, the way they do in the theater, or get whisked away by nannies, the way they do in English novels. Somebody has to be taking care of them every minute of every day for years and years and years.

If you are a plain, or full-time, housewife with children, it begins to feel like jail, except that in jail you'd at least have grownups to talk to, and maybe pick up some nifty tips from the hookers.

If you are a housewife with children and a job too, sooner or later the twain shall meet.

CHAPTER TWO

For a long time I called myself an advertising copywriter. I was still, of course, a housewife. Except for the statistically insignificant handful of single women living in full-service hotels, we are all housewives, but it was nice to put "copywriter" when filling out forms.

I had a marvelous time. I was one of the lucky ones. A lot of women who work spend their days typing other people's letters, where at least they get to sit down, or checking out groceries in the supermarket, where they don't, and aside from the money the only good thing about it is that they aren't home, which is nice; two lives are better than one. And they have someone to talk to. All that lovely gossip and scuttlebutt and gripe.

Now that I am a full-time housewife, I talk to myself, and the cats, and the dog, but it isn't the same. Very small children following you around wanting to use the Windex may give you the illusion of conversation, but they aren't what you'd call people, and when your husband comes home he wants to watch the news. For the entirely housed mother, whole weeks go by when your discourse consists of only the following lines:

Go back and wash them again.
Well, what did you do to *him?*
Brush your teeth.
Put it back where you found it.
Get out from under my feet.
No, you've already had three.
Are you sure you brushed your teeth?
Where does it hurt?
Use your napkin.
You're going to spill your milk.
Stop splashing in there and get washed.
Go to sleep.
I said *no.*
Why don't you go watch television?
Don't run with the scissors.
Pick it up.
Hang it up.
We have to wash it so I can see where the blood's
    coming from.
Are you sure you don't have any homework?
Wash the *backs* of them too.

Conversation is almost reason enough to go get a job.
I had what is known as a creative job, in what we re-ferred to, giggling, as the Glamorous and Exciting World of Advertising, and a scrungy lot we were, too. In the

beginning I dressed for work, but when the younger generation came sweeping in with their rumpled jeans and shaggy hair, the rest of us felt overdressed, and stopped combing *our* hair too. After a while, the boss caused a partition to be built between us and the front offices where all was hush and carpeting and the muffled buzz of phones, and he kept the door shut.

Back where we were herded in, in steerage, so to speak, it was not felt necessary to have carpets or windows or even four-legged desks, and it became a convenient place to store things like leaky water coolers and spavined file cabinets bulging with ancient mail. We all slopped around together in there brewing coffee and telling stories and putting up rude signs. We spent hours of company time inventing complicated advertising campaigns for imaginary products. We invented an intimate masculine deodorant called Cock-a-lura, and papered the walls with elaborate layouts and discreet, insinuating copy. We threw papers on the floor. We brought in lunches of leftovers in plastic containers, and heated them by thrusting our gooseneck lamps down into the containers until the offices reeked like a soup kitchen. The cleaning women stopped visiting our quarters. Advertising may indeed be a glamorous career, but somewhere else, not there.

It was rather the way boarding schools sound in books, but probably aren't, and we cavorted wickedly behind our closed door while the bosses brooded on the other side like grownups. In our hysterical relief at packing in the Christmas rush, we chased each other up and down the halls with cans of spray-on snow.

Nobody called me Mom. Nobody called me Hey, as in, "Hey, when's dinner?" I felt very cozy and solid, being called by my rightful name again, the way it was when I was young.

However, it could hardly be said that I had gone forth into the real world to shoulder my responsibilities as a fully adult citizen. It was only too plain that I had left my responsibilities behind, in the dubious hands of a series of baby-sitters and cleaning women, who whiled away their time moodily stuffing the silver spoons down the garbage grinder and frightening my children of policemen and thunder. As soon as my foot touched the doorstep of home the hired help scattered like starlings, and the children swung from my arms and rummaged in my pocketbook and complained, and there was dinner to get (meat loaf? spaghetti?) and clean up after and the laundry to fold, and I was grown up again.

I failed to rise in the business world. When offered promotions and manly responsibility, I ran screaming from the building. Who goes to work to be responsible? Plenty of people asking me questions after I get home.

Because of my complex erratic life I was brutally underpaid, which had its advantages. Irreplaceable at half again the price, I came and went freely, and when called into the boss's office for a reprimand, instead of standing neatly in front of his desk as he liked to see us, I hitched my bottom onto a corner of it and lounged, and said, "Yassuh, boss." These perquisites didn't count for much at the grocery store, but they cheered the heart.

I argued rudely with clients, and refused to take my

lunch-time turn at the reception desk, and I brought in little children. I had to.

Emily started her office career early.

That was the year I had a wildly unreliable baby-sitter. She was sick a lot, and her friends kept calling in to say she couldn't come today. Toward the end, I was lucky to see her two days out of five. She was a listless sitter and an apathetic apartment-tidier, and I only kept her because she was so pretty. I thought she could be the first black Miss America. Entrepreneurial visions danced in my head. I told her that if she would stop trying to subsist on white bread and sliced American process cheese, and take the lovely vitamin and iron pills I gave her, and stick with me, babe, I would make her fortune.

She only smiled wanly.

Finally I did fire her, but in the meantime I learned how to get a baby carriage in and out of an elevator without becoming separated from it at the wrists, and Emily went to a lot of meetings, where she made noisy comments and cut her teeth on the boss's keyring. I learned how to take notes around a lapful of baby.

One of my bosses of the time had a recurring nightmare about his employees drinking on the job. I don't know why, or whether it had ever actually happened, but he thought about it a lot, and after hours, when everyone had gone home, he crept around the deserted offices looking for whiskey bottles in our desk drawers.

In my bottom right-hand drawer he found a plastic bag full of wet diapers.

I GET A MORE RELIABLE SITTER, BUT NO ONE'S PERFECT.

Emily grows, and graduates from carriage to stroller, and from stroller to fat legs, upon which she insists on pushing the stroller, now containing my pocketbook. She will be pushed no more. Being pushed is no way to travel in a strange land; you have to get out and mingle with the fierce reality of it, running your hand along the gritty bricks, stooping carefully down to pat the dog turds.

At this point in the city child's life, mothers are frozen into stasis, able to see but not to move, as if embedded in lucite. Gone are the pleasant Saturdays in the park. We never get as far as the park. It takes an hour to go around the block, even with the short cut down the alley.

It seems impossible to proceed that slowly without actually standing still. Every flight of front steps must be solemnly climbed, and then inched down again, backward. The littered dirt around every tree must be inspected. Every empty soda can and cigarette butt must be picked up and marveled over, with little murmurs of appreciation.

"Put it down," I say. "Dirty."

"Birdie," she says dubiously, looking around, puzzled, at the middle air.

"Not birdie. Dirty. Nasty."

She stares down at the spread starfish of her fingers, and then wipes them obediently on her shirt. "Birdie," she whispers.

These days, when I have to take her to the office, I sometimes splurge on a cab. It's worth it.

I am husbandless at this time, and the three of us, me and Emily and the sitter, roll up together in a warm ball of utter femaleness, soft as a two-year-old's pink flannel sleeper, cooking and singing and combing our hair and drying our underwear over the shower rod. We slop around over coffee cups, and I heat up endless cans of chicken noodle soup. If all the chicken-flavored noodles we consume during this time were knotted together, they would reach to Pittsburgh. I was raised on the stuff myself, and it seems the proper food for little girls, mild and comforting.

The only male in our woolly nest is the cat.

It was time to get a cat. I had an apartment and a job and a baby, and now I needed a cat. A cat is a sign that your traveling days are over. You are standing still now, and can stop having those dreams about missing trains, and about buses that climb up and up a steep drawbridge that touches the sky, with a strange city spread out below you, and then at the top the bridge is open, and half a mile beneath you there's water, and ships.

A cat means you have scrabbled out a little piece of the world to be home for the time being. You own a comfortable chair, and a refrigerator.

Emily and I went to the SPCA. We inched respectfully past dogs that looked as big as ponies to Emily, and with much sharper teeth, and came to a wire-mesh enclosure simply crawling with kittens.

Seeing us, a black one detached itself from the tangle and scrambled over the others and shot up the side of the cage shrieking. At the top it clung, spread-eagled, exposing the thin-furred pinky-purple skin of its armpits, and screamed. It was looking me right in the eye with a glittering urgency. The other kittens, wrestling or napping or washing, were perfectly content. This one wanted out, and I was its chosen liberator. Its voice assaulted the ear, and now that I looked more carefully there was something different in the whole kitten. It was speaking purest Siamese, and except for being coal black, it *was* Siamese, the alley genes thrust under and the Eastern heritage stamped all over it, small oval paws and wedge-shaped head and long pointy string tail. It continued to scream Thai threats and imprecations after me while I hurried obediently to find the attendant.

He detached the claws from the wire mesh. "Don't you want to know whether it's a boy or a girl?" he inquired.

"It doesn't matter," I said. "That's the one."

"Funny. Most people care." He upended the squalling, flailing kitten. "Boy," he said.

And Boy he was.

He moved in like a bull in a beauty parlor. He roistered around and climbed the venetian blinds and knocked over lamps. He took wild kamikaze leaps onto the table and landed in bowls of chicken noodle soup. He fell into the bathtub. He tore the books out of the bookcase trying to climb in behind them. While the plumber was wedged into a crawl hole considering some pipes, Boy gave a scalp-shriveling Siamese war cry and scrambled up his back onto his head. He ate the mail. When company came, he lurked on the hat shelf in the closet waiting for them to hang up their coats. He fought with my stockings and slept in my bed.

Emily, impressed by this rampant male presence in our quiet life, decided to become Boy. She referred to herself in the third-person masculine as a cat.

"He's not Emily," she said. "He's a kitty. He's a baby kitty. This is how he drinks his milk." She bent over her cup until the wispy tips of her pigtails brushed the table, and tried to drink with her tongue. She walked on all fours.

CAT AND CHILD GROW.

At the office now she sits in her own chair at my desk and draws pictures with felt-tip markers from the art department.

One of the bosses comes in. "Hello! I didn't realize we had a nursery-school division here!"

"I didn't have anyone to leave her with. My sitter has the flu."

"Sure, sure. It's a pleasure. Hi, honey, what's your name?"

As if he doesn't know. By this time.

Emily scowls murderously.

"She's shy."

"I am not shy. I just don't like him."

I don't either.

"Ha, ha. I think my secretary has a box of candy, and she'd just love to give a piece to a pretty little girl like you. I bet you like candy, don't you?"

Emily shakes her head.

"Sure you do! All little girls like candy."

"He's not a little girl. He's a kitty."

"Tell you what. You come with me, and we'll see if we can find you some."

"No."

"Go on, Emily. Don't be a goose." I clench my teeth.

"No."

"Well then, I guess she doesn't get a piece of candy. She'll be sorry."

Scowling blackly, Emily bends over her drawing. The felt tip squeals with pressure.

To me, he says, "If I could just see you in my office for a minute, about the Rittenhouse campaign," and leaves.

I get up. Emily gets up. "No, baby, you stay here. I'll be right back."

"I'm coming too."

"But I'll only be a minute. You stay and draw. Finish your nice picture."

"I'm coming too!" She attaches herself tightly to my clothes.

The boss is less pleased to see her in his own office.

"She didn't want to be left alone," I mutter lamely.

"Yes, well. Look, they've cut back the budget for fall. We're going down from spreads to pages, and they'll be black-and-white. We're dropping color till the spring presentation."

"Emily, put it down! Sorry. Emily, you mustn't touch things on other people's desks."

"Oh, she's all right. So we have some new layouts here, and I thought perhaps a different copy approach . . ."

"No!" I smack Emily's hand and put the fancy clock

back. Unstrung, Emily begins to weep. The boss's secretary looks in, surprised. I pick Emily up and hold her. She kicks me. I would like to cry myself.

"I'm sorry," I say. "Yes, you were saying, a different copy approach?"

Why am I always apologizing, what have I done wrong? Am I a criminal, that I have this job and this child?

ON SATURDAYS WE TAKE OUR CLOTHES AND A BOOK TO the laundromat. Emily puts the quarters in. I hold her up while she pours in the soap, slowly, watching. The machine jerks and shudders and begins to churn. We sit on a bench there and I read to her. The other people on the bench slide their eyes around to us and then away again, trying politely not to hear. I read our way through the *Just-so Stories*, pronouncing in a loud clear voice, " 'Vantage Number One,' said the Bi-colored Python Rock Snake," while the other people study the signs on the walls about not using dyes or obscene language. I read *Peter Rabbit* and *Tom Kitten* and *Squirrel Nutkin* and *The Tailor of Gloucester,* all those little square green books with the fragile, faded pictures.

We pile our damp wash into a shopping cart and transfer it to a drier, and put our dimes in. Our clothes tumble around like birds. Emily bends her nose on the window: "There's my shirt. Look, there goes my blanket!"

The laundromat is warm and steamy and feels cozier than our own apartment. Home is where the wash is?

There was ironing in those days. Back home, I iron,

and sing tunelessly to myself. Emily sings, and chatters quietly, and litters the floor with blocks and crayons and picture books. As each thing is inexpertly finished I put it on a hanger and suspend it from something handy. The chandelier and the bookcase and the doorknobs blossom with our shirts and dresses. The iron hisses on the damp patches and the room smells delicious, like biscuits in the oven.

SOME BOSSES ARE IDIOTS AND SOME ARE CRAZY, AND some are kind of attractive.

There was one in particular. We told each other our troubles. He liked me because I was poor; he thought it was a matter of principle with me, an ascetic, rarefied approach to life. It wasn't. It was because he didn't pay me enough, but I didn't tell him that. Occasionally we would glance at each other, sideways, in a speculative way, wondering, what if . . .

A lot of trouble, though. Marvelous how in books and movies people, even people with small children around, simply drop into a nearby bed when the spirit moves them.

One evening he needed some work from me in a hurry; I forget why. Going to meet a client at dawn? At midnight? Anyway, I went to his apartment. Not being somebody in a movie, I had to take Emily with me.

This boss was newly divorced, and newly moved into a fancy penthouse in a cloud-capped apartment tower down by the river. The elevator took days. Weeks. I held Emily's hand for comfort.

You stepped into the apartment and it was all glass,

and you could see for twenty miles in all directions, giving you the impression of having gotten off the elevator in the wrong place, into nothing at all. Air.

I crept closer to the glass walls and looked, still hanging onto Emily. God's-eye view. Streets and highways pouring light. People turning their lights on in Pennsylvania, New Jersey, and Delaware. There was my city, all of it. There was the river winding away toward the bay, and the ocean. On your left, Guam. I wanted badly to sit down on the floor. If there was a floor.

My boss brought me a martini and I drank it.

"Listen," I gabbled. "Is it my imagination, or does this thing . . . this place . . . *sway?*"

"*Sway?*" he shouted. "Are you kidding? Remember that storm last Tuesday? With all that wind?"

"No. I didn't notice."

"I suppose not, in your brownstone, but let me tell you, there was a *wind*. And this place didn't sway, it *rocked*. Look at all that glass. Windows everywhere. I was sure it was going to go. Blow in on me. Cut my head off. I'm telling you, I haven't been so pants-wetting scared since the *war*. I took a chair and I got in the elevator and I went down to the *lobby*, and I *sat* there. I just sat there in the lobby till about three in the morning, and then I came back up here and put a mattress on the kitchen floor and slept there. It's the only place the glass can't get you."

I thought kindly of my poor boss, crouched in the stark red and silver lobby, holding his head in his hands to keep the glass from cutting it off. It occurred to me, again, that it might be very nice to go to bed with him.

"You haven't seen the bedroom," he said, clairvoyantly.

From the bedroom you could see Waycross, Georgia.

There was a fur rug on the floor, and a fur bedspread on the bed. Fur sheets, probably.

"I don't see how you can sleep with that view."

"I put the pillow over my head."

We stood there together contemplating the fur bed. After all, why not? Consenting adults, unattached . . .

"I want something to drink too," said Emily. She pulled gently on my wrist. "And I'm hungry." Then she saw the fur rug and threw herself down on it and rolled and rolled deliciously, like a puppy, laughing.

We gazed down at her. Lock her in the closet? The refrigerator? The elevator?

Well, no.

I went to the kitchen and got her a glass of water, with ice cubes in it to make it more satisfying, and looked for something for her to eat. Crackers, maybe.

There were shelves and shelves of glasses in matched complete sets of all sizes; presents from his old cronies. In the refrigerator there was half a bottle of cocktail onions. There was nothing to eat.

Ah, well, presently some girl would move in with him, and hang heavy curtains over the glass walls, and put orange juice and eggs and butter in the refrigerator, and roister around in the fur bed with him. Some other girl, not me, alas.

In the living room my boss and I got out the layouts and did some work. His hand, pointing, brushed against mine, and we both snatched our hands back, and then laughed uneasily. Emily poked around the room crunching ice; from time to time I looked up and told her not to touch things.

I am Emily's mother, I told myself, keeping count, and this man's employee and would like to be his lover, and an advertising copywriter, and someone else who turns up mostly in nightmares and is afraid of elevators and the view through glass walls.

I took Emily back down the elevator and across the lobby, and we walked along the windy river to a restaurant, where I ate bouillabaisse and Emily ate a shrimp cocktail and was rather imperious with the waiter. I thought, what an odd way to live. What an odd *mixture* of ways to live. It's not that I would trade in any pieces of it, only I do wish they would fit together somehow.

CHAPTER THREE

E mily sleeps in the bedroom and I sleep in the living room, and the kitchen is the kind where you're always stepping in the cat's dish and kicking over the garbage bag. The top layer of the garbage bag, the part that spills, is where the coffee grounds and cigarette butts are kept. The cupboard doors creep open, and hover, waiting, until you bang your head, and in tears of rage and pain you slam them shut so hard they bounce open again, and you bang your head again.

"Don't you want to take your bath?"

"No. He's a kitty. He hates baths."

"Maybe he's the kind of kitty that likes baths?"

"No." She brings the hairbrush, and I'm supposed to sit still. "I will make two pigtails," she says importantly. "You have to hold still. Now lean your head this way. I won't hurt you."

I slip into one of those spaces of inertia where the world stops moving. The late afternoon sun comes in through a crooked venetian blind and throws its crooked stripes on the bookcase and wall. Boy crouches on the window sill, glaring down at pigeons, his sharp Siamese shoulders poking up. I suppose there are street sounds, horns, voices, air conditioners, sirens, but we are city folk and don't hear them. The tap in the sink drips, the refrigerator labors. It needs defrosting. Downstairs in the vestibule someone rings a doorbell, someone else's doorbell, and presently the answering buzzer unlocks the front door, and feet climb the stairs, past our apartment, on up. I close my eyes.

Emily turns my head this way and that, and tangles my hair with the brush. "You have to hold still," she says, in my voice. "Or I can't make two pigtails for you."

I FIND A NURSERY SCHOOL THAT PROVIDES TRANSPORTA-tion. A driver will come by and pick her up at eight-thirty, and return her at twelve-thirty, to be received and fed by the sitter.

The arrangements are okay, the school is okay, Emily is amenable, but the whole thing comes as something of a shock to me. For me to leave her and go to work is not the same as her leaving me. Not the same as her climbing out of our private world and going off to be a public child, somewhere else, among strangers. It makes me nervous.

Now every morning I put on my high boots and my coat, buttoned up to the chin to conceal a peach-colored nightgown edged with beige lace. Emily and I go down-stairs to the vestibule. I carry a cup of coffee with me and cuddle it in my hands for warmth, and keep one booted foot jammed in the inner door so it won't click shut and lock me out. We wait for the school car.

We have joined the great world. All over the country, mothers and children are waiting for school cars, school buses.

One apartment in our building opens, not into the hall inside, but directly onto the vestibule, with its doorbells and mailboxes. Mrs. Lowry lives in there. When she hears me wrestling with my mailbox or my key, or now, when she hears us chatting in the mornings, locks scrape, and the door creaks open on its two-inch chain and a narrow slice of Mrs. Lowry's face appears.

"Peekaboo, Mrs. Lowry."

She doesn't speak. She never does. Every weekday morning at eight-thirty we are here, Emily and I, rain or shine, but every morning Mrs. Lowry seems to hope we are not us but something else more interesting. I taste my coffee and wait for the door to close and its locks to scrape shut again. I don't like her door being open. Something might get out through the crack, something invisible but nasty, like a smell, that she's keeping in there.

Emily ignores her.

This morning the car is late, which usually means we have a substitute driver, lost somewhere and peering at his list of addresses. The regular driver is okay but has other irons in the fire that tie up his time (white slavery, maybe, or pushing smack) and then he sends a substitute. This worries me. I mentioned it to my friend Helen, mother of Linda, and Helen laughed. "That's because Emily's an only child," she said comfortably.

At last the horn blows. Emily tugs open the outside

door, but I can't see who the driver is from where I am an-chored, by the foot, to the inner door. Friend or stranger? You have a child, and then you shoot it out into the world like a paper airplane from a high-up window, and it will have to learn to float, like me, on air currents and faith. If you lose your faith you fall. Everyone knows that.

I go back into the building and let the door crash shut behind me.

Shower. Dress. Beds. With a heave and a thump my own bed vanishes and my bedroom is a living room again. Pack lunch while eating toast. Note for the sitter. I am late again. I am always late. You'd think they'd get used to it, but they don't. Bosses poke around looking for me as if I might be hiding in a file cabinet, under C for copy-writer, maybe. Or H for housewife. M for mother. Then they leave a sarcastic note on my typewriter for me to find when I come in.

I leave work early too, every day, and every day they are as grieved and astonished as an abandoned dog. Al-though I have never missed a deadline, never failed to de-liver in full with every word neatly typed, rightly spelled, a feeling is growing around the place that I am basically unreliable: sometimes there is no one in my chair. I could get a doll made. One of those blow-up plastic ones. Dress it in my clothes.

At work, I write a stack of radio commercials for a men's wear store. They proceed automatically from brain to fingers without thought. In the beginning I used to have to time the things, whispering them to myself, enunciating ve-ry clear-ly and watching the second hand on the clock.

Now the shapes of the sixty-second, thirty-second, and ten-second spot have sunk down into the dream-deep centers of the folded brain and seep from there to the finger muscles. I am never wrong. Curious talents we pick up on the road of life. Not like a rolling stone but like rolling Silly Putty; junk embedded forever, along with the names of presidents, and how to tie a half-hitch, and what to do for croup.

Our clients are a mixed bag of retail stores and small manufacturers whose ads are full of the oddest information, delivered in hysterical tones: "NOW! We Can Supply Our Clients with Copper or Stainless Steel Grommets in ALL Sizes from ⅜ inch to 1 ⅝ inches!"

LEADERS OF INDUSTRY
RELY ON WHITBY'S REINFORCED CABLE.

The ad dances tantalizingly in my head; portly leaders of industry dangling over a cliff, hanging from Whitby's cable, chatting affably and drinking martinis.

No way. They want a photograph of the cable, probably. Ever see a photograph of a cable? And then, if there's room, a photograph of Mr. Whitby, stern, with jowls. That'll fetch 'em, every time.

SPRING DRESSING: FLOUNCED AND FLOWERED

20% OFF ON ALL SUITS, SLACKS, AND SPORTCOATS

HERE'S HELP WITH YOUR
INDUSTRIAL SCREENING HEADACHES

Not dignified or important work, but easy enough, and

I support us, myself and Emily and Boy and a portion of my sitter's family.

I like coming here. I have friends here. We sit on each other's desks to eat our lunch.

Xeroxes and memos and layouts and stacks of copy and leftovers of lunch and melting cardboard coffee cups. From the art department, the cheerful stinks of rubber-cement thinner and fixative spray. Typewriters. Phones.

Phone for me.

It is Helen, mother of Linda. "Listen, I just called to make sure Emily got home from school all right."

"Why, of course. I mean, sure, my sitter would have called me. Why?"

"Oh, I'm just so mad and upset I can't think. We had a substitute driver again today, I guess you noticed. Well, when he delivered the kids home he didn't ring the doorbells. I guess no one told him to. He just opened the car door and left them on the sidewalks and drove away. At least, I suppose that's what happened, I can't get it straight from Linda. So of course she couldn't reach our doorbell, or even read which one was ours even if she could reach, and after a while I guess she just wandered away. The police picked her up at Twelfth and *Lombard*. Five blocks. And think of the *traffic*. She's never crossed a street before."

"Oh, Lord. Oh, Helen. Is she all right?"

"She's fine. The police gave her an ice cream cone. Okay, I just wanted to check on Emily. I have to hang up now and faint."

I sit looking at the phone for a while. Then, reluctantly, I pick it up again.

My sitter answers. "Now, isn't that funny? I was just fixing to call you. Here it is something to two and Emily not home yet. You think anything's wrong?"

"Oh. Oh, but you can't mean it. And you didn't . . . Listen, go outside—no, don't. Stay there, somebody might —I'll be home in twenty minutes, you stay there."

I hang up, and dial the police emergency number. It rings, and rings, and rings, and rings. I sit and hold the phone because I don't know what else to do. The second hand on the wall clock moves majestically in its orbit.

Startling me, a brief cross voice answers. I explain, and he writes it all down: blue coat, red hat, red mittens, white tights, brown shoes with buckles. And my address. I have a lot of trouble explaining why I am not there, at my address, but somewhere else, and spend several minutes telling about Helen's phone call, and my job, and my sitter. He seems anxious to get everything absolutely straight and correctly spelled before he does anything rash.

I do not scream. It is important not to start screaming.

He will send a squad car to my apartment. I will meet it there.

Never mind the elevator. I push my arms into my coat while running down the clanging iron back stairs. The bus. The bus will save time. I stand at the bus stop, but there's no bus in sight. After several minutes I turn and run up the street to the next bus stop, one block closer to home. This is stupid but gives me something to do.

The bus comes, and I ride standing bent down to look

out the front window, knees flexed like a skier. At my corner I leap off into the gutter, and the squad car is parked in front of my building.

One of the policemen comes up with a notebook. No one has told him anything except the address. The information I gave the other cop was strictly for office use. This one starts over again, with the brown shoes and the red hat and the blue coat and the white tights and Helen's phone call. He is wearing heavy gloves and writes with considerable difficulty.

"And your age?"

I tell him, like a good girl, and then cry, "Are you *crazy?* What does my age have to do with it?"

He seems hurt. "I'm sorry, ma'am. I don't make the rules. I have to get this information from you."

It is important not to scream. See how *he* isn't screaming, see how calm he is, and the other policeman, his cohort, how he leans back against the side of the squad car as if he might never move again. I want them to scream. A very small girl is lost and alone somewhere in this city, and I would like everyone to scream, please. At least to run up and down the streets shining searchlights into dark passages and shrieking their sirens.

The street is empty. I was expecting it to be full of people walking dogs or carrying groceries; people I could ask, people who would help me look. No one. Like a street on Mars.

"Okay, ma'am, I guess that's all." He closes his notebook and strolls back to his car, revolver moving rhythmically against his hip.

What is he going to do? Anything? What am I going to do? I run a few steps down the street, past my building, and then stop and turn back. Should I be by the phone? Has someone called already? Does my sitter know anything? I run up the front steps.

As soon as my hand touches the outer door I hear her, and yank it open.

She is lying on the floor of the vestibule with her cheek on the filthy tiles. Little square tiles like a bathroom, once white, never washed. She is crying with the scrape and shuddering gasp of someone who has been crying for a long, long time, and has no real sobs left, just the spasmodic jerk of stomach muscles.

I drop to the icy floor. She has wet her pants, and her clothes are soaked and freezing. She is cold as stone. "Oh, baby. Oh, baby, baby, baby."

She wrestles for breath. "I cou—I cou—I couldn't—" The muscle spasms choke her off.

I drag her onto my lap. "I know. Hush. I know." I look at my watch. Almost half-past two. Two hours.

Two hours. Two hours calling in the cold outside the locked door of your home.

For a child, ten minutes is forever.

Bolts scrape and chains rattle. Mrs. Lowry's door creeps open an inch and an eye appears in the crack.

"Mrs. Lowry," I cry, "were you *there?* Why didn't you let her in, she's been here so *long.* You could have rung our bell. She couldn't reach. Just rung the *bell* for her. You heard her crying."

After a minute she speaks, and I hear her voice for the

first time. "I didn't like to interfere," she says. "I always mind my own business."

I lurch to my feet, dragging Emily with me. "You ugly old *bat!*" I am crying now myself, but for once instead of subsiding in shame I simply shout over my own tears. "I hope you break a hip! You're all alone in there, and I hope you break your hip in the bathtub. I hope you slip, and lie there and cry for help in the bathtub and just keep lying there and crying and nobody ever comes and I hope you *starve to death* in there!"

It is an awful, awful, unforgivable thing to say, and I have never said anything like that before or since, and I feel somewhat better. For a moment, anyway. Then I remember that it is not Mrs. Lowry's child; it is my child, my fault. My paper airplane that fell.

The crack closes, the bolts rasp back into place.

It's too much trouble to dig for my key, so I ring our doorbell. It is fully twelve inches above Emily's highest tiptoe reach.

My sitter comes to the top of the stairs as we climb them. "Thank the Lord you found her," she says. "I've been half worried to death."

Behind her, from the open door of our apartment, the rattle and crash of studio laughter rolls out like a bag of blocks falling. If she had just gone down to look out at the street. Stare up and down the block to see if the school car was coming. If.

I turn off the television. "You can go home now. I won't be going back to work."

Emily's teeth are chattering in her filthy, swollen face,

and spasms still shake her like hiccups. I strip off her wet clothes and roll her in a blanket while the tub fills. Pneumonia starts with a fever. Fever and cough. Pleurisy is a sharp pain in the chest. Oh, Emily, Emily, why didn't you *tell* him you couldn't reach your doorbell? No, how could she? He was the grownup and she was the child confided into his care to take whatever sudden or mysterious thing he gave her; how could she ask, any more than the paper airplane asks the air? Emily, Linda, Marshall Thorpe, Eric Lindsey, Shelley Kaplan, all standing abandoned on their sidewalks, unsurprised, as the car turns the next corner and disappears.

I set the cup of cocoa on the edge of the tub and tie her hair up with a ribbon. "Drink that carefully," I say. "Take little sips until it gets cool." I arrange the plastic ducks and boats around her.

My knees are quivering. I sit down on the toilet and watch her, and after a while her teeth stop chattering and the spasms subside.

If I were Emily I would never go to school again. I would never leave the *house* again. But she is made of sterner stuff, and dresses herself the next morning without comment.

At breakfast I promise her, over and over, that always, every single day, rain or shine, someone will be waiting for her outside when she comes home. *Outside*, on the front steps. But she is being the baby kitty again and only meows at me, and pokes her tongue down into her orange juice.

INSTEAD, IT IS I WHO BEGIN TO BE AFRAID OF THINGS. I wait for the light to change, and check my breasts for cancer in the shower. I get up in the night to make sure the door is locked. When Boy coughs, I take him to the vet. I am not so clever as I used to think, and there are things out there waiting for us to make the wrong move. Get off at the wrong bus stop. Buy the wrong package of salami.

I am like a high-wire artist in the circus who has ridden a unicycle for years, way up there in the crisscrossed light beams, and now I look down for the first time and see all that space down there, waiting with its mouth open, and all those faces; they look like Mrs. Lowry.

We need more ballast up here, for balance. Another person, maybe.

I begin to think about getting married again.

CHAPTER FOUR

There are things you forget about being married. One is that you must always check for the toilet seat before you sit down. It's hard to remember, in a hurry or in the night. Another is that you can't serve chicken noodle soup for dinner any more.

The leftover ham, creamed, with rice? How long would it take the pork chops to thaw? I could cheat and put them in a warm oven. Potatoes? Macaroni? Spaghetti? Paprika, cinnamon, roach spray?

Boy disapproves. My new husband says, "Does that damned cat have to sleep with you like that? It's obscene." Boy purrs and closes his eyes, ignoring him, and buries his claws in my shoulder with possessive love; he was there first. My husband stands over us, hands on hips, and glares down at the bed.

My husband hates our apartment and I hate his, and in any case there's no way the four of us would fit in either one, so we buy a house.

It is one of five tall thin new houses squeezed together in a tiny alley way downtown. The rest of the alley is dirty

and dilapidated but has a kind of perverse urban charm.
Our house contains thirty-nine stairs, with a couple of
rooms on each floor, like living in an elevator shaft, and it
is fragile but pretty. We settle in, and have some shattering
fights about furniture. Friends come to see us, and we all
sit around on cartons of books and chat.

My husband says, "I suppose if we're going to have
a baby we ought to get started."

"Mm," I say.

The next morning I think it over and change my mind,
but the next morning is too late.

I really like being pregnant. It makes me feel
amiable and rather sleepy. In fact, I fall asleep whenever I'm not actually in motion. My only problem is that
I find it hard to connect pregnancy with babies, and quite
impossible to connect babies with sex. I do not, basically,
believe in the facts of life, and no wonder it's so hard to
get them across to children. No wonder they give you that
incredulous stare. Santa Claus and all them flying reindeer
are a cinch to swallow, compared to the facts of life. I
think there are primitive tribes around to this very day
who don't believe a word of it, and it wouldn't surprise
me if they were right. The whole thing's an absolutely epic
non sequitur. Can you possibly imagine any two things
with less connection, less in common, any two things more
stubbornly incompatible, than sex and babies?

I go along with it, though, reluctantly, like the Church
finally faced down by Galileo, and paint the fourth floor

room for Emily to move into, and borrow a crib. My husband, in a burst of atavistic superstition, dyes some curtains blue and hangs them.

I get enormous. It makes them nervous at the office. Whenever I waddle in, they boil water.

"WHAT?" SAYS MY MOTHER, ON THE PHONE. "THAT'S impossible. I don't believe it."

"It's true. I saw the X-rays. Like what's left on your plate after you've eaten a couple of trout."

"Well, well," she says. "Twins. Well, well, well."

I BORROW ANOTHER CRIB.

If one baby is hard to believe in, twins are a joke. Twins are a hospital-waiting-room cartoon from an old *New Yorker* album. *Real* people have a baby. A baby. Twins are silly. Take any context of high tragedy or history or drama, and stick twins in it; and directly you've got a farce.

"Once upon a time there were twins, and they looked so exactly alike not even their own parents could tell them apart. Well, when the time came for the twins to marry . . ."

Also, there is definitely something nasty in the thought of the same person happening twice; it strikes deep at the vitals of self-respect. *I* happen to be unique. If I have no other use on earth, at least I am irreplaceable; no one else is like me or ever will be. Whereas a twin must be worth only half as much as a single child, since no unrepeatable combination of genes is lost to the world if one of twins vanishes. Twins are a waste of space. Nature could have used the same energy and area to scramble up a different magic combination of trait and temper and nose and chin, all so inexhaustibly various that repetition seems absurd.

None of my friends has twins. No one in my family has ever in recorded history had twins. I do *not* think it is cute, nor would I like it any better if I did. Frankly, I have never really believed in twins, any more than in the facts of life. I thought twins were invented, and pretty implausibly, too, by Shakespeare for some of his sillier comedies, and perpetuated ever since for the sole use of bedroom farce and the limpest of children's books.

It is absurd to lug around in your immense lap something in which you do not believe. I felt the same way I did when my husband and I saw the UFO; insulted, that they expect me to believe such poppycock.

I sulk, which does not, of course, have the smallest effect on the impending arrival of the twins.

I get a book on twins from the library, and Emily and I sit and study the pictures, with me holding the book on my knees, at arm's length. Between me and it, the twins turn somersaults and have fist fights and I try to ignore them. The book leaps.

Our friends think of a lot of frightfully funny things to say.

Since I was working, I had felt entitled to a decent wardrobe of maternity clothes, and treated myself to some pretty snappy outfits. By four months I had outgrown most of them. By seven months there is only one left I can wear, a sort of army tent, and I wear it every day, gloomily. It looks tired. If this goes on much longer I shall have to cut armholes in the bedspread.

I walk to work every day, and in the street people glance covertly at me and speed up a little as they pass, just in case.

After seven months, apparently there is simply no more room in there, and the twins decide to look for larger quarters.

SINCE NOBODY HAS OFFERED ME SO MUCH AS AN ASPIRIN, I think I might as well make the most of my lucid state and watch. No such luck. The first thing they do is take away my glasses, without which I can scarce tell night from day. I might as well be watching reruns of Dr. Kildare, or an educational film on polar bears. All I can see clearly is my own knees, and I can see those any old time.

My husband has been underfoot all day, so the doctor lets him come in and watch. *He* can see. I do all the work, and he gets to watch. He has brought along a *New Yorker* to hold over his face if it gets too revolting. A lot of other people have dropped in to watch too. People hustle around in the blur, and fuss with incubators, and keep giving me oxygen. There is a clock on the wall so enormous I can actually read it; it says ten after eight.

The first twin arrives, and is weighed in and popped into an incubator. "Boy," says the doctor.

"How much?" asks my husband.

"Two pounds."

"Good God," says my husband. "I had more than that for *dinner*."

One down, one to go. A figure in the blur pitches a bucket of antiseptic at me from the far end, and it sloshes up along the table and soaks into the roots of my hair.

The second twin has to be yanked out by the scruff of the neck, like a kitten down a well; the doctor has him out before I can collect a good shout. Another boy: identical twins. This one weighs four pounds and a bit.

I manage to push away the fiddling idiot with the oxygen and holler, "Wait, I want to SEE!"

Reluctantly, just for a flash, they show me something wrapped in a towel, and then whisk it away. It looks exactly like my husband's father, who is eighty. My father-in-law, after processing by one of those interesting tribes along the Amazon. Good old J. J., he's always disapproved of me and here he is again, *twice,* pickled and withered and shrunken but unmistakable.

They rush the incubators away.

My husband floats into focus. "How are you?"

"I'm fine." I am, too. That's certainly one thing to be said for childbirth: when it doesn't hurt, it doesn't hurt. Stops instantly. In between labor pains, and immediately after, it's gone. No other pain can make that statement. "I want a cigarette."

My husband lights and hands me a cigarette. All over the room oxygen tanks are hissing like snakes. People leave suddenly. We are all alone. I feel very, very empty. "I'm hungry. I didn't have any dinner. I didn't have any *lunch.*"

People come back and courageously wheel me and

my cigarette out of the room. (How was I supposed to
know oxygen is explosive, for pete's sake; what am I, a
chemist?)

The hospital kitchen is closed, of course. Hospital
kitchens are always closed when you're hungry; they open
only when nobody wants to eat. Six in the morning, before
you've brushed your teeth. My husband goes out into the
world foraging, and comes back with a hamburger and a
bottle of beer. They put me in a room with a woman who
has just had her fourth boy. They were so hoping for a
girl, but figure they'll give up now. My stomach brushes
against my spine, I can move easily from side to side in
bed, I weigh 112 pounds.

That was Friday. Monday morning I leave the hospital
swinging my pocketbook in one hand and a basket of
daisies in the other.

The twins seem very far away. Even with my glasses on I could hardly see them, stowed away in the back
room behind the nursery, in Isolettes. A pair of orphan
baby rhesus monkeys. The keeper's wife will raise them
on a bottle for me. I am anxious to see Emily; I feel no
connection with the twins at all.

From what I hear and read, every other woman in the
world is simply awash with maternal sentiment from the
moment of conception on, and only I am peculiar and
heartless. Even for the seven months that they were, so to
speak, house guests of mine, I didn't have any more *personal* feeling for them than I do for my gall bladder. There
is definitely something wrong with me. Or else everyone
else is lying. The moment they departed from my premises

they were taken over by the hospital, which seemed like a swell idea; I took my daisies and went home, and slept soundly all night. If I'd known how I was going to need sleep later, I'd have slept for weeks.

The next day, I go to the office and pass out cigars. It's supposed to be a joke, sort of.

The office is horrified. The boss's secretary keeps saying, "But we just sent you a *card*. To the *hospital*. Now you won't even get it."

The women in the office lower their voices and sympathize with me. "It must be just awful for you, having to leave them there like that. Just horrible. I can imagine how you must feel, you must be so *worried*."

I blush darkly, and try to feel the way they can just imagine I feel, but it's no use.

My boss comes out of his office and yells at me. "What the hell do you think you're doing here? Get out. Go home and go to bed. No, wait, I'll call you a cab."

He's right, actually. I do feel a little shaky in the legs. Coming was just a joke, a silly gesture of bravado, and now I feel definitely weak, and sit down on the edge of someone's desk to wait for the cab.

But I take some work with me when I go.

LIFE ASSUMES A SORT OF SPURIOUS NORMALITY. EMILY and I wait on the front step for the school car in the morning. I make the beds and go to work. In the evenings, we call the hospital to find out how much the twins weigh; when they weigh five pounds they can come home.

The head baby nurse adores them. They've stayed and

stayed; she thinks they're hers; other babies come and go but the twins stay on. She talks about their personalities as if they were people. I hold onto the phone, and nod and smile at it, and try to sound interested. "Aw, isn't that cute? What else does he do? He does? And how much does the other one . . . I mean, Benjamin . . . how much does he weigh today?" It isn't easy to remember that these are mine, not hers, we're talking about.

We're supposed to visit, too. I get the impression that we're expected to get a sitter for Emily and come every single evening and stand there in the hall, gazing over the baskets of real babies through a second sheet of glass into the back room, into the plastic bubbles of the Isolettes at our own little worms, who look like an antiabortion poster. We manage once or twice a week.

I catch myself cooing at the real babies, so much closer and more appetizing. There's one little blond in particular, with fat pink cheeks like a Della Robbia angel. And another, a dark little Irish pixie. My husband pokes me. "You aren't supposed to be looking at those."

The Isolettes have flanges in the sides with rubber gloves sealed into them. The nurses shove their hands into the gloves and do inscrutable things to our babies. "Which one is that?" says my husband. "The one she's fooling with?"

"How am I supposed to know?"

He looks at his watch. "It's been five minutes. Do you think that's long enough?"

"Better make it ten. We haven't been here since Tuesday, they think we're awful."

"The movie starts at eight, and I'm going to have trouble parking."

Slowly, half-ounce by half-ounce, the twins grow.

It turns out the hospital is holding them for ransom. Getting them out is going to cost the kind of money I thought existed only in Kipling stories, moldering in lost cities, great rotting sacks of gold splitting and spilling out rivers of coins over the rubies and emeralds in the dark, with the white cobra keeping guard.

"We could sell one," my husband reasons, "to pay for the other."

We drain the savings, sell the stock, and appeal to our various parents. My husband figures and figures on little scraps of paper, and sighs and shakes his head. "There's no way. They'll just have to keep them, that's all."

I have a mental picture of them at six or seven, living in the hospital, playing with the wheel chairs and racing each other down the long halls. Doing their homework in the waiting room. Learning to read from *Today's Health*. "Try again."

Somehow we finally manage to bail them out and bring them, first Ben, then Matthew, home. Which, as my husband says, was our second big mistake.

LIFE DROPS INSTANTLY INTO A STATE OF PERMANENT crisis, like life on an everlastingly sinking ship, or in an eternally burning building.

In the book Emily and I read, it said that husbands were always charmed by the idea of twins, and rallied round to help take care of them, quickly becoming expert in the art of juggling one while diapering the other. Unfortunately, my husband hadn't read the book. He wasn't charmed at all; he was horrified by the fuss and noise, and seemed to think it was all my fault. He never went near the babies. Indeed, he pretty much stopped speaking to any of us.

I hire a practical nurse, and someone to do the vacuuming. Emily retreats to her attic room and stays there most of the time, puttering quietly with crayons; I still manage to read her a bedtime story, though my head occasionally drops onto my collarbone in a sudden passionate fit of sleep.

The bigger twin, Benjamin, is an easy baby, the kind that isn't really born until it's several months old. He wakes, howls, drains a bottle, soaks his diapers, and sleeps again. A creature of pure function, he has only traded a crowded womb for a crib.

Matthew, the little one, is sickly. His screams go leaping through the house like flames. He lives in a car bed, so the nurse and I can carry him around and keep him nearby, cutting down on the running and the stairs. He fights being nourished; an ounce of milk, two ounces, and he jerks away as if it was turpentine, and his shrieks rend the welkin. Every three hours around the clock, for months and months, we try to feed him. He screams now when he sees the bottle. We fiddle with the formula, trying this and that. The doctor suggests paregoric, which offends him so fiercely he stiffens and turns dark purple with rage. The nurse tries scotch on him instead; it seems to help a little. She eats dinner with us, one hand in her lap, where Matthew lies belly-down across her knees.

On weekends the nurse goes home and sleeps.

Babies are supposed to be fun. Emily was fun. I played with her toes and made her giggle, and blew noisily into her tummy and made her laugh and squirm. In order to enjoy a baby you need a few extra scraps of energy and spaces of time. When, for six or eight months, three uninterrupted hours make a full night's sleep, you do not play with anything or anyone. Life is pure survival. You can't even say, "Look! I got through the day!" because there is no end to the day. It goes on all night.

I work ninety hours a week, and am on call the rest of the time. I am constipated: no time.

Staggering out of the laundry room at one in the morning with a basket of piping-hot shirts, I wonder dazedly what there is I can *stop* doing. There must be something I don't have to do.

We must all eat.

Food has to be bought and cooked and cleaned up after.

The babies must be taken care of around the clock.

We must all wear some sort of clothing.

Emily, thrown almost completely on her own at four-and-a-half, still must have some kind of minimum care and feeding and washing.

Do I have to go to work?

Well, I am earning nearly half the family income, but even so it seems as if working is the only thing I can decently abandon.

I don't, though. Work is my haven and refuge and vacation. The office is often chaotic, but compared to home it's a tropical isle covered with palm trees.

I set out for work in the mornings, on foot, reeling slightly with exhaustion along the broken sidewalk, and my spirits begin to lift. The sun is shining on the red bricks of Philadelphia and the window-box petunias and the gingko trees, and the taxis are yellow as buttercups, and everyone is going to work, hustling along with brief-cases and morning papers, and I am too, and the public world is an orderly place where we each go arrowing along the streets toward our daily tasks. We whisk through revolving doors and into elevators. We say hello and good morning to our comrades and sit down at our desks.

Free!

It's odd, but at home, where I literally hold life and death in my hands, I feel helpless. Desperate, confused, incompetent, exhausted, powerless. While here at my desk I feel important. I sit here and write an ad for a sale of men's suits, so that some man who almost certainly already *has* suits can dash off and save 20 per cent on some more, passing money from his wallet to the wallet of our client, who will go straight out and pass it on to somebody else. That's the entire purpose of my job, and most jobs: to keep the money sloshing back and forth from A to B and back to A again. Every time it changes wallets the government gets a piece of it, so they can build interstate highways and pay Congress. It's rather like a playground game, with a circle of kids and a ball.

All that money moving around makes it seem important,

but of course it isn't. Not important the way it's important to get an extra ounce of milk down my older son, which is what I ought to be doing.

I feel guilty.

I do love it, though, and I refuse to give it up. Perhaps what it boils down to, I blush to admit, is that here at the office I can ball up a piece of paper and fire it at the wastebasket, and miss, and leave it lying there on the floor. Somebody else will pick it up. Or if they don't, it doesn't matter, it's none of my business. Not what I'm here for.

This, then, is what it feels like to be a man instead of a housewife: missing the wastebasket and leaving it there.

It's heaven. I feel guilty, but I will not quit.

I go to bed in my bathrobe, because I got bored with putting it on and taking it off all night. I lie stiffly in bed, poised to leap and run. Boy no longer sleeps with me. My night life is too much for him. He sleeps downstairs, on the couch, with his arms wrapped around his ears.

My husband sleeps, it seems to me, defiantly. The louder and more frantic the household gets in the small hours, the more solidly he sleeps. It is nothing to do with him. He refuses to involve himself in anything so disorganized. Lazily, easily, he rolls over and resettles himself in his pillows, and sleeps on.

I think occasionally about killing him, but I'm too tired. I don't have time.

I spend countless hours on my hands and knees in the dark feeling around under the cribs for a pacifier.

If I turn on the light, it will wake up the other twin.

Pat, grope, feel. There's something. The pacifier? Ugh, no, something else. Yes, of course I have an extra pacifier; it's the extra one I'm *looking* for. Dust woozies. Doesn't she ever vacuum in here?

Maybe it's stuck between the mattress and the bars of the crib. It often is. I work carefully along the bars like a blind nun telling her beads. Nothing. The baby screams and screams, the other baby sleeps; it will wake up later, in an hour or so. They never both scream at once and then both sleep at once, so I can sleep.

Maybe it bounced when it hit the floor; they do. Maybe it's way over here. I crack my head on the corner of the bureau and start to cry, and then trail off because it's too much work, and besides it's no use; no matter how long I cried no one would come to take care of me, and say "Don't cry," and pick me up and carry me to bed and tuck me in and let me sleep. Nobody would ever come. Sniffling with self-pity, I pat and feel my way along the edge of the rug. Then suddenly, surprisingly, my face is on the rug and I am asleep, my back end still propped up. The wires let go and drop me down and down into the waters of sleep. My arms and legs evaporate like mist. Sleep buries me like the weight of mountains. Eighteen inches from my head my son is screaming fit to shatter glass, but for thirty seconds or maybe a full minute I sleep like the blessed in a feather bed, my face pressed into the rug.

Emily wants to take the twins to school for Show and Tell.

Summer, fall, winter.

Matthew weighs thirteen pounds and begins to be

reconciled to life. Decides to stick around, and to eat, bitterly, the minimum necessary to do so.

Ben is all dribble and spit and smiles and tears and drenched diapers; a juicy baby.

Christmas.

I SIT IN THE SORT OF HIGH-STRUNG TORPOR PECULIAR TO this day. The floor is deep in wrapping paper and babies. My husband and Emily crouch over a little square blue metal loom upon which it is possible to make, with loops, thousands upon thousands of pot holders. "Here, let me," he says. "I remember these things, I used to have one." She moves over to make room for him and watches solemnly.

Benjamin has focused on his favorite chair. At this time it is the joy of his life to make his way over to it and wedge himself tightly underneath it, and cry. He balances on his hands and toes and pitches forward, landing with an audible flump. Back onto hands and toes, pitch forward again, flump. A beached whale would be more graceful, and make better progress. It is Ben's only method of travel.

I have built a Christmas fire. We have a fireplace, one of those shallow ornamental city fireplaces, and for seventy dollars a man comes in a truck with a couple of dozen sticks of wood, which he pitches contemptuously into the street in front of our house. Horns honking around us, we gather it up and carry it in, through the front hall, up the stairs, across the living room, and out onto the balcony, where we stack it in a small neat pile. We burn it reverently, like incense.

My husband has completed his first pot holder. It is only so-so.

Matthew lies on his back on the floor. He is a rigid baby, without movable joints, and appears for the moment to be part of the Christmas mess, a carved wooden doll, souvenir of somebody's travels in the Tyrol. Then he stiffens and points his toes and rolls, quick as a flash, over and over until he is under the Christmas tree; this is Matt's only method of travel. He pulls a silver ball out of its holder and inspects it, lying on his back, murmuring comments. He tastes it. Lousy. Pinches it. Then slings it across the room. "*Da da da da da da!*" he shouts. We all jump, and he giggles.

Boy, reverting to kittenhood, starts to chase the silver ball, and then recovers himself and stops to wash. He has already eaten his catnip mouse, and moves now with the ponderous, slow-motion care of a dignified drunk.

Ben has managed to get his forequarters wedged under the chair and tunes up to weep. "Ning, ning, ning," he mourns, muffled. Emily hauls him out by the heels.

Our immaculate brand-new house with all its furniture so tastefully chosen by my husband is beginning to look tired. There are whitish spots on the carpet where milk has been spit by creeping babies. There is a baby bottle on the mantelpiece among the Christmas cards. There are ragged areas on the arms of the couch where Boy has vented his disapprovals.

I feel rather shabby myself. I got up too early.

The phone rings; friends want to come over for a drink.

I look around, but only briefly, at the Christmas mess.

I will not clean up. I won't. It is nearly a full hour before I have to feed the twins again, and I am not going to do anything at all till then. That is my Christmas present. That, and the earrings I am somewhat painfully wearing, and a perfect imprint of Emily's right hand, immortalized in clay and painted blue.

The friends come in, crunching empty boxes and scuffling paper, and my husband gets out bottles and ice and sets them on the table, on top of a thousand-piece jigsaw puzzle of an English garden and one of those drearily educational board games for ages four to eight, about the principal products of various states. Ben has found a ribbon to eat, and it has leaked red all over his chin.

We all wish each other a merry Christmas.

"Ought to clean up this mess a little," says my husband.

Before I can stop him, or maybe I don't even want to stop him, he has gathered up an immense slippery armful of wrapping paper, ribbons, cards, and boxes, and stuffed it into the fireplace.

Fantastic. Great blossoming flourishes of flame. They leap roaring out of the tiny fireplace into the room. All the long rows of Christmas cards on the mantelpiece spring into the air and are sucked into the flames; camels, snow scenes, Santas, wreaths, barns, candles, Currier & Ives, pine trees, stars, "Hope you can visit us in Louisville in the coming year," the whole works, like a flight of burning birds.

Ben rocks back and forth drooling with delight.

I am suddenly moved to save us all, and jump up and throw my drink into the blaze. Glass and all.

My husband is pounding up the stairs, I suppose to get a glass of water from the bathroom.

As abruptly as it began, it's over. The fireplace is choked with ash and the ghostly remains of foil paper, which doesn't really burn. Mummies of Christmas cards eddy around the room. The smell of smoke blends with the piny smell of the tree, and there are charred spots on the carpet, and some broken glass, and a shadow of smoke on the ceiling.

My husband comes back and we all sit down again. He makes me another drink, in another glass.

"Well, cheers," say our friends.

"Cheers."

"Cheers."

Next week is the end of this year. I have survived, Matthew has survived, all of us have come through and the worst is probably over. I smile dimly around at the mess. Tomorrow Christmas will be finished and I will be safely back at the office again.

CHAPTER FIVE

We bid a loving farewell to the baby nurse, and take on an ordinary sitter who will, while the twins nap, reluctantly run the vacuum cleaner and break the dishwasher and stack the Sunday papers. This leaves my spare time free for the irregular jobs, like cleaning the refrigerator. Waxing the dining room floor.

I use Johnson's paste wax because that is what my mother used, and I do it on my knees, leaning on one hand, rubbing with the other, because that's the way it's done. I like the smell. Late at night, after the dinner dishes and Emily's story, I crouch my way with infinite slowness and patience across the dining room. Noisily I move the table and chairs to one side, and crouch down again. It's a long job.

My husband, passing through on his way to bed, thinks I'm insane, and he may be right. But I do this because this is what people do, this is what my mother did. We had a maid (lots of people did in those days) but my mother waxed the floor herself, on her hands and knees, and we all tied rags on our feet and skated around to polish them.

No one here is left awake to tie rags onto, so I knot them around my own feet and slide solemnly back and forth in the middle of the night, with Boy sitting upright on the gerbil cage watching. No doubt he too thinks I'm nuts. However, this is the way it's done, and I do it.

Clearly I am not the stuff of which progress is made. I think wistfully sometimes about radical women, the dedicated rule-breakers, the fierce, driven, single-hearted women who have set aside their own lives and comforts in the passionate interest of change. I would like to have been born like that. I wasn't. For me, there is a sensuous pleasure in repetition. I carefully recreate my own childhood for my children, and my mother's life for myself, and I settle myself on Emily's bed the way my mother did on mine, and I read, "It was seven o'clock of a very warm evening in the Seeonee hills when Father Wolf woke up from his day's rest." I pronounce "Seeonee" and "Akela" the way my mother did. Presently it will be time to start the cycle again for the boys, and I will read, "Flopsy, Mopsy, and Cottontail, who were good little bunnies, went down the lane to gather blackberries." The inflections are my mother's.

I want to scrub the bathtub with Bon Ami, pronounced "Bonn Ammy," but it seems to have gone off the market. What are they trying to do to me, anyway?

Housewifehood is creeping gradually over me like moss on a brick path, overlaying the remnants of my girlhood. Even my desk at work is neater than it used to be, and I throw away yesterday's Styrofoam coffee cups.

In my odd leftover bits and pieces of time (six in the

morning, one in the morning) I do little things for my house. Scrub the greasy city grit from the window sills. Paint the living room. Take all the books down and dust them and put fiction in the living room and non-fiction in the study, an arrangement that evaporates immediately, since its continuation would depend on nobody ever reading anything. I wire-brush the rust off the balcony railing and paint it. In the dark sour little square of back garden, with Boy pacing along the top of the fence, flipping the end of his tail and telling himself jungle fantasies, I try to plant things; they gasp and die. I dig in drawers and closets and throw away a lot of things that either climb out of the trash in the night and go back to the closets again, or else have been instantly replaced by other, similar things.

I surprise my husband with a new shower curtain. Surprise and appall.

THERE IS A FLAT SPOT IN THE LIVES OF BABIES AND mothers, at about ten months; the novelty has worn off but the baby is still there, no longer a surprise and not yet interesting in its own right. You gaze upon its downy head and dimpled fists, and you are bored blue.

Later, it learns to walk and talk, and its person-ness expands and takes up more and more airspace, and the house feels crowded.

One child is an appendage. More than one is a way of life.

One child is outnumbered. You can brainwash it. You can make it do what you want it to do, carry it to parties and toss it on the bed with the coats, lug it in a backpack through the Adirondacks, teach it to say "How do you do?" and pass the hors d'oeuvres. Plural children are a counter-culture in the house. You and your husband are outnumbered. A creeping, irresistible tide of Legos and Lincoln Logs and doll clothes and Matchbox cars seeps into the living room and cannot be turned back. You no longer go to New York for the weekend, you go to Disneyland instead, and dine at six instead of seven or eight. You pack up everything and move because the schools are better somewhere else. You spend long hours in social converse with people you would never otherwise have met at all, because your children know their children.

Relentlessly, year by year, you are pushed backward, shouting helplessly, from your own life into theirs. Your own errands are wedged into the time left over after you've taken the children somewhere and brought them home again. When they get older, you're lucky if you get to use your telephone one try out of six.

With one child, you and your husband are still yourselves; you have merely acquired an extra thing, like a Yorkshire terrier or an electric toothbrush. More than one and you're a family, and the piano keys are covered with jelly and whenever you try to talk to each other somebody says, "Who's he? Do I know him? Why is she going to divorce him, doesn't she like him any more?" and after a while you give up.

I have read that it's terribly important to a healthy marriage that the wife set aside some quiet private time to chat with the husband, preferably when he gets home from work, or they get home from work. Just half an hour. Peace, privacy, a couple of martinis, and "How was your day, dear? Is the new man working out all right?"

I would like to get my personal hands on the people who keep suggesting this, and find out how I'm expected to manage.

"Now, I want everyone to play quietly and nicely in your rooms for half an hour, while Mommy talks to Daddy."

"I want to talk to Daddy too!"

"Later, sweetie. Right now is going to be our private time together, and then later you can have a private time with him, okay?"

"What are you going to talk about?"

"Oh . . . I don't know. Things. Now you play nicely and don't interrupt us, all right?"

"What if it's something important?"

"It better be terribly important."

Peace. Privacy. The well-chilled martini.

"And how was your day, dear?"

"Well, as a matter of fact—"

An ominous splintering crash overhead, and you both glance apprehensively at the ceiling. Silence.

"As a matter of fact, something rather interesting seems to be brewing. Scott was saying—"

Feet on the stairs. A child, and another child behind it.

"I said not to interrupt us."

"You said if it's important. It's important, I have to ask you something."

"What? Ask, and leave."

The eyes unfocus, the face blurs, the sneakered toe traces a pattern on the carpet. "I'm trying to remember . . ."

"Hurry up. Mother and I were talking."

Theatrical hand on brow. "I can't remember. I've forgotten. It was important, though. Can I taste your drink?"

"No. Go back to your room."

"Just a tiny *taste?*"

"Go upstairs and play!"

Bitter looks. Feet stomp halfway up the stairs and then stop; silence, not even a breath, in case of missing a single word from below.

"Yes, well, you were saying?"

"I forget. Well. Did *you* have a nice day?"

Muted scuffling on the stairs.

"Oh yes. Very nice."

You gaze at each other, paralyzed with self-consciousness, each wondering how you came to get stuck with this doltish stranger. Besides, it's time to start the water for the spaghetti.

There's always bed, of course, but mothers of more than one child fall asleep with startling suddenness and finality.

You could write each other notes. At least until the children learn to read.

Some parents communicate in high school French, but my husband took German instead.

We take to calling each other at our offices when we have anything to say.

THE TWINS ARE OLD ENOUGH TO PLAY IN THE ALLEY.
Allowing for the inevitability of dog shit, the alley makes
a nice small filthy cheerful playground. There are other
children. There are tricycles with which to run over other
people's fingers, and gingko trees, and a high old wooden
fence to somebody's yard that leans dangerously out over
the broken sidewalk, bulging with vines. Emily found a
dead rat to play with. Lean, slat-sided cats move about
their business, and vanish into the boarded windows of
an abandoned house. Its blackish brick walls have been
decorated with spray paint, saying PEACE and FUCK and
CornBread and JM.

I sit on the front step, with the door open into my
house behind me to save taking a key, and beam at all
this. I know most of the people who pass down the alley,
and say hello, and glare at the ones leading large dogs in
here to our sanctuary for evacuative purposes.

At the far end of the alley the Cat Lady presides. We
have been speaking cordially for years now, and it's too
late to ask her name. She is white-haired, black, built like
a ship, and stands there with her arms folded looking
formidable. She was here originally. We are the new folks
in the new houses. If you find a stray kitten and can't
scratch up a home for it, she will take it, calmly, unsmil-
ing, in her capable hand, and say, "It can just go in with
the others," and disappear into her house.

The children play, and cry, and are called back from
the dangerous main streets at either end of the alley, and
dig in the filth around the gingko trees where I planted
crocuses once, in a fit of irrational optimism.

There are playgrounds within walking distance, and sometimes my sitter, Mrs. Jackson, finds it worth while to take the twins to them so she can sit on a bench and chat with the other sitters. The alley is better, though. Playgrounds are too big and violent for small children, who can't reach the drinking fountain, and get bowled over like ninepins by a stray basketball or a sudden scramble of big kids, or beheaded by swings.

Besides, it's hard to get to a playground or anywhere else with twins. It was hard enough with Emily; with two it's impossible. I go to a pet store and buy two large-dog harnesses, red, and matching red leather leashes, because while you are rescuing one twin from the wheels of a bus, the other is throwing itself under a truck. *I* think the little harnesses and leashes look very spiffy; they don't speed up our progress any but at least I know where both boys are at any given moment. However, I get a lot of angry comments from passers-by. People seem to feel leashes are an offense to human dignity. So are twins, actually.

I come home from work and turn into my alley. The twins come running to greet me with their mouths open. "Look," they gargle proudly, pointing to their tonsils, "no chewing gum!"

"Of course not," I say briskly. "I told Mrs. Jackson you weren't to have chewing gum. It's bad for your teeth."

We go through this routine for many weeks before I smell a rat: Mrs. Jackson, herself a passionate chewer, has been giving them wads and wads of gum with strict instructions to swallow it as soon as I turn the corner into the alley.

In the event of thunder, or even dark clouds, there are no twins in the alley, no Mrs. Jackson. I unlock the door of my house and go in. "Hello?" I call. "Mrs. Jackson? I'm home."

No answer. No one downstairs in the kitchen, or upstairs in the living room. I go up another flight, to the bedroom floor. The door of the hall bathroom is shut tight.

"Hello? Mrs. Jackson?"

A small voice: "We're in here."

I open the door. Mrs. Jackson and both boys are crouched under the basin, squeezed into the narrow space between the pipes and the toilet. Mrs. Jackson unwraps herself and stands up, brushing off her skirt. "We heard some thunder," she says with dignity. "The boys were scared."

The boys continue to crouch.

"That's silly, thunder can't hurt you. It's just a noise. Come out of there."

"That's what I told them. Thunder can't hurt you. They wanted to come in here anyway. There aren't any windows." She laughs lightly, and glances around at the protecting walls.

SMALL BOYS ARE NOT THE SAME AS HUSBANDS. YOU DON'T have to grope for the toilet seat to make sure it's there. It's there, all right. Somewhere under the pee. Mop before sitting. *Why* aren't there urinals in private houses, why, why? Or at least a ladies' room and a gents'?

The diaper pail vanishes from our lives.

The high chairs vanish. So do the phone books, on which Matthew is sitting at the table, and the *Columbia Encyclopedia,* under Ben.

The housewife's journey isn't something you can figure on a map, tracing it along a marked road with a crayon: job, marriage, first baby, second baby, first Cub Scout pack meeting. It's more like a series of rooms. The passages from one to another are always dark, and rather mysterious, and mostly you can hardly find them again later. You just look up one day and you're in a different room. Different furniture, different view from the windows.

One day you're standing in front of a washing machine feeding it diapers and setting it to pre-rinse. A week later you're in there digging in pants pockets for crayons and lollipops, and the next day it's pencil stubs and pennies. From there, I suppose it's only around the corner to condoms and car keys, and then there will be only your own clothes, with grocery lists in the pockets, and your husband's, and you'll hardly see the laundry room at all. The scenery rips past you. It has something to do with the dizzy speed at which children grow, and you don't. Relativity.

The boys start nursery school.

Emily starts first grade and rides a school bus instead of a school car, and I take time off from work to go to spring concerts and Christmas concerts and, later, a play in which all the other children are adjectives and nouns and adverbs and Emily is a dog. She is a marvelous dog. She spends a lot of time on all fours anyway, a kitty no longer but a horse known as the Famous Hum.

(Hum isn't famous *for* anything, actually. Just plain famous.)

Time passes, in orderly and predestined fashion at the office and by fits and starts at home. Occasionally my sitter, being mortal, gets sick, and leaves me with the boys on my hands when nursery school shuts up shop at noon, and home and office meet, producing deep cracks in the substructure of the latter. Matt and Ben learn to use the intercom, and the adding machine, and the water cooler. They learn to use my desk chair, taking turns; one child spins the other around and around till it's dizzy and then hurtles child and chair rocketing down the hall into the art department, followed by a crash, and shrieks.

Later, when they learn to use the elevator, things get quieter.

The Cat Lady gives Emily an ugly slat-sided alley kitten with patches of white and patches of stripes and a talent for the heart rending silent meow. Emily names her Betsey. Betsey grows up and gets pregnant and gives birth to four hideous kittens, on our bed, an hour or so after we get home from a late and riotous party.

The kittens live in a box in the laundry room. Betsey is happy beyond belief. They are just what she always wanted. She looks up at me, blinking in the light, and curls a forepaw around the little nursing worms, and purrs, and is so plainly in pure heaven that I feel rebuked. I can't remember being so utterly soaked in bliss with any of my own young.

Later she gets sick of them. We give away all but the black-and-white one with the crooked Hitlerian mustache.

His name is Sidney. Now we have three cats. Or, rather, two cats and Boy.

The furniture looks a little worse with each passing year, and the type of toy you step on in the dark changes, and the balcony railing needs painting again. The stairwell is covered with fingerprints. I wire-brush the railing again, and paint the stairwell, and wax the dining room floor by night because this is the house we live in, and somebody has to take care of it.

*I*t's a nice house, but you can't see the sky. You can climb all the way up the thirty-nine steps to Emily's eyrie, and from there you can see the sky; rooftops, chimney pots, sky, and a glimpse, in winter, of the statue of William Penn on City Hall. If you don't want to climb clear up there, and you need to know whether it's cloudy or sunny, you crouch down by the sliding doors in the dining room, almost to your knees, and lay your cheek against the glass and twist your neck and peer upward, and from this complicated prayerful attitude you can see a slice of sky the size of your two fingers, blue or gray.

From the windows at my office I can see bricks and buildings, and the windows of other offices where somebody is bent over digging something out of a file cabinet, or answering an inaudible phone.

I get pneumonia, and go to the hospital.

I am very sick, and spend eleven days there. It's a lovely old hospital, broad and gracious and generous, in red brick; a motherly looking hospital. It gathers me into its

lap, and from my bed I can see the sky. Sky, and part of a
tower with a greenish roof and a weather vane. At night
planes crawl across the black, twinkling for a landing. By
day it's often blue. Sometimes snow falls out of it, harmless as feathers past my warm bed. I lie there and curl and
uncurl my toes, and cough delicately, painfully, and watch
the sky.

The nurses are marvelously kind. Late at night, when
the new shift comes on, one of them will stick her head
in to see if I'm awake, and if I am, she'd be glad to fix
me a milkshake. After I'm asleep, they tiptoe in and rotate
me gently, so as not to put too many needles in the same
place. Beside me the IV stand is like a guardian angel,
although something of a nuisance at times; we have to go
to the bathroom together, and there's an infuriating little
lip at the bathroom door that I have to boost my guardian over.

At home, the children are certainly squalling and arguing. Probably there's no change for milk money, and we're
out of cat food, and someone has flushed the hairbrush
down the toilet, and nobody has clean socks, but there
is nothing, nothing, nothing I can do about it. I curl my
toes with satisfaction. For the first time in years there is
nothing I am expected to do for anyone. I am a patient.
It is my sacred duty to lie still and look at the sky, and
receive needles into my flesh, and get well. I am not even
responsible for feeding myself. Glucose moves with infinite slowness into my left arm. If they would give me a
catheter, there'd be nothing at all I need do.

People come to visit, and sit with me, and I am polite

and try to look grateful but they are an interruption. I was busy. They come bumbling in smelling of cold weather and the great world, bringing news about other people whose names I barely remember, and then they sit there, wishing they were somewhere else, because they hate hospitals. Finally they go away, and I reseal myself into the warm circle of sky and glucose and attending angels.

Sometimes the office calls me, but they're very respectful and don't suggest that I do any work, because I am not only sick, I am in a *hospital*. They speak on the phone with nervous reverence, and urge me not to worry about a thing. I don't.

My mother has come to stay at my house, and see the children get to school in the mornings and try to dig the hairbrush out of the toilet. She brings the children to the street corner at a prearranged time to wave at my window. I get out of bed, trailing my IV stand, and lean across the air-conditioner and wave. They stare wildly from window to window, and finally see me, and wave back. Then, bored, they turn away, and Mother takes them around the corner out of sight. I crank my bed up a little and get back in it and settle down, with my face to the sky. It is very pleasant.

After a time I feel stronger. I read *The Blue Nile* and *The White Nile*, pausing in my reading for long intervals to lie and watch the sky. I feel lighter than air; I might float off the bed, melt into the sky.

"Wow," everyone says, when I am home again. "I bet you're glad to get out of *there!*"

I AM HOME FROM THE HOSPITAL, BUT BOY REFUSES TO speak to me. He sits with his back to me, and won't answer. I touch him, apologetically, and then snatch back my hand; he's filthy. The once-elegant close-grained satin-black fur with blue glints has not been cleaned since I went away, and is dull and sticky with neglect.

He will not speak, he will not turn his head to look at me, but he knows I am back. He begins to wash. He washes all over, starting behind the ears and working methodically clear to the tip of the tail; it takes nearly an hour.

ANOTHER THING ABOUT HAVING MORE THAN ONE CHILD is that you're supposed to move to the suburbs. All our friends did. Now, when we want to visit them, instead of walking around the corner we have to take a train, and when we get there they show us the pine-paneled family room and the greenness of the bluegrass, and talk about the excellent school just two blocks away.

Possessed by apathy or a childish reluctance to leave the streets of our youth, we stay in the city with our three children. At parties, we play a game called School, which is played between teams of snobs and teams of liberals. (This was the sixties, when people inspected their social consciences with the same tender intensity that in the fifties they gave to their mental health, and in the seventies to their sex lives.) The snobs brag about having their children in the best and most expensive schools available, and the liberals about having theirs in the worst available. It ends in fisticuffs.

Our fragile house shakes and splinters to the patter of little feet. Every time the neighbors are burgled we buy a new and more elaborate set of locks, bars, and chains, which has no perceptible effect on burglars entering but will certainly prevent anyone's leaving in case of fire.

Every Sunday afternoon friends telephone to say, "The agent's name is Trager. Are you writing this down? It's only five minutes from the station, and it's got four bedrooms and two and a half baths and a pine-paneled family room."

We make writing-down noises in the background, ask an intelligent question about the furnace, or the grade school, and then go tell the children that if they will stop shinnying up the floor lamps and jumping on the piano we might take them to the park later.

The suburban friends rarely come to visit us, and never after dark. They read the papers, they know what it's like in town.

But once in a while, on a Sunday afternoon when the sun is blinking through a poisonous haze without, and within the children weep with loneliness and boredom and the Sunday papers lie all over everything like a fall of dirty snow, we begin to wonder.

We get the car from its garage four blocks away and drive out of town to look at houses.

After crossing a vast waste of shopping centers laid end to end as far as the eye can see, we come to a place where there used to be a chain of little towns; they have melted together now. Schools here are a point of competitive pride, and houses have windows on all four sides.

Indeed, houses *have* four sides here, instead of only front and back. With our local guide we drive up and down the pleasant streets, dodging dogs and soccer balls.

We grow quieter, and after a while all conversation stops. There is a peculiar melancholy here, in the autumn dusk, with the silhouettes standing against the smoky leaf fires, and the strange isolation of the houses on their separate squares of grass, and the children's voices thinning in the growing dark. Life here seems like a kind of exile. The houses feel like houses on a Monopoly board, in danger of sliding off. The people here seem to inhabit a blank space a long way from the heart of life, and the clean air smells of leaf-smoke and mortality. The moon detaches itself from some trees and looks down, and, looking up, we wonder how it would be if that weren't the moon at all but the earth, with its familiar outlines of continents and seas turning slowly in the black sky a long way off.

Some boys practice basketball shots beside a garage, and I am unreasonably moved by them, as if I could see them doomed by some terrible premature decay, probably lurking even now in the dark bushes by the driveway. Lights go on in kitchens. Voices call children to supper.

We go home again, back through the waste of shopping plazas.

The stern yellow owl-eye of the City Hall clock watches us down the length of Broad Street. Philadelphia seems to radiate a kind of sturdy cheerfulness. The trees in their concrete tubs outside the Fidelity building have more grace and courage than suburban trees. The Union League squats soberly, and something is happening at the Academy of

Music, and the dowdy Philadelphia rich emerge in minks and dresses made out of old antimacassars, and climb into limousines of marvelous antiquity.

Past Frank's bar. Antique shops. The serious long-haired young striding up and down all night in jeans. Our own dear alley, loud underfoot with broken glass and soft with the deposits of enormous dogs, or mastodons. We're home.

We say to our few remaining friends in town, "Are you going to join the new swim club?"

"No, we're moving to Chestnut Hill."

"Is Sally going to McCall's School next year?"

"No, we're moving to Elkins Park."

When we need a little fresh air we close all the windows. Everything we own except the house itself, which is pretty heavy and we don't really own it, has been stolen at least once.

Liberal friends in Abington and Bala Cynwyd envy us the richness of our children's lives, exposed so broadeningly to the poor, the criminal, and the Art Museum.

The city belongs to us. It gives us solidity and strength. Walking to work in the morning, walking home from the theater at night, when the commuters have all gone home, we take possession of our streets. We watch, critically, as things are built and torn down along our regular foot trails. We walk past hospitals and houses and office buildings, garages, bars, stores. We live here. Our footsteps ring out sternly with ownership. No one can own a suburb; suburbs come in privately owned pieces.

Riots sweep through town. Our suburban friends

admire our courage, or pretend to; secretly they think we're nuts. The truth is, we simply draw our cowardice from an older source than newspaper headlines. Man's a lonesome animal, and it's cozy, at six on a winter evening with the smell of snow in the wind, to pull your city a little closer around your shoulders, glance back at the wise eye of the City Hall clock, and set off for home down your own streets and alleys. It's cozier than striking out into the long darkness looped and strung with red taillights toward the edge of the world. After all, cities are the primal seed of civilization, calling this lonesome animal to huddle together with others in a single cave, and build one fire for all of them. And those lone families, in the separate caves way over there, are the outcasts, beyond the reach of the firelight, out where the dragons are.

We hold out longer than anyone else.

ALL WINTER, WALKING TO WORK, I FIGHT THE HEADWIND on Seventh Street, a mean filthy wind that scours itself into the roots of the hair and pours through coats and sweaters. My eyes stream tears and grit. Blown newspapers wrap around my ankles. The lid of a trash can bowls crazily along the gutter. I long and long for summer.

Summer comes.

Summer doesn't last very long, and you have to use it while it's there. I put the children to bed and take a drink and go out to sit on the balcony.

Our balcony is just wide enough for a wicker chair, and just long enough for two wicker chairs. I sit in one.

There are five of our houses together here, and each

has an air-conditioning unit out back. Across from us is the side of an apartment building, and each apartment has a window air-conditioner. The noise is astonishing; I can hardly hear the buses going by on Lombard Street. I can smell them, though. This is one of those weighty Philadelphia evenings when smell doesn't rise, it packs down, and spreads. Old Philadelphians can separate the smell into its component parts: bus, and coal gas, and the oily breath of Marcus Hook, and a week's sidewalk accumulation of dog shit, and the careless garbage cans of the apartment building. The smell seems almost as loud as the noise. Surely it's worse than last year? Maybe someone has stuffed a corpse into one of the garbage cans, and left the lid loose?

The back area here is walled on all sides by the backs and sides of buildings so the air-conditioner roar is trapped, and booms back and forth. Air-conditioners drip slime down the apartment walls in front of me. The air they keep pouring at me is wet, and stirs my hair, a disgusting, damp, hot, noisy wind made of the breath of strangers and the smells of their dinners.

This is the summer I waited and waited for.

Suddenly, the city that I had thought such an affectionate and merry place to live feels like a dead rat full of maggots, and I want to get out. Just for a minute. Just to see the summer.

THE COUNTRY WOULDN'T BE SAD, LIKE THE SUBURBS. Country isn't a place cast out by the city, but has a life and reasons of its own.

If we had a place in the country, my husband and I could sit at our respective desks at three on a Friday afternoon and think, by six we'll be there. Breathing leafy air, pressing our toes into the grass, and the children catching frogs in the creek. If we had a shack in the woods, or an old crooked farmhouse in an abandoned orchard, we would sit around the kitchen table in the evening and listen to the bugs batting against the screens, and the children would leave their muddy shoes by the door, and the cats would go out hunting.

I would grow tomatoes.

I think more and more about the country, and it swells up and takes over my whole mind, like love, and absorbs both my lives. I go to the library and take out books about people who moved to the woods, or bought old farms, or renovated log cabins in Maine, and maybe there was a lake, or an owl, and I become obsessed with these books, until their gardens are my gardens and their owls hoot in my sleep. Waking up, every morning I am surprised by the sound of traffic instead of roosters. I subscribe to *Organic Gardening,* and move through the crowded streets at lunch hour in a daze of composting and mulching.

I know there's country west of the city somewhere. We've never been there, but you can see by the map that it's country; there aren't any roads to speak of. I convince my husband, and we pack the children into the car with some picture books and Cracker Jack and drive west of town looking for a place.

None of the books told me what I was really driving toward. What was really out there.

They didn't say I was headed straight for the bubble gum on the bathroom rug.

Those moved-to-the-woods books, and the readers' articles in *Organic Gardening,* had implied that there was no *inside* to their houses. They spoke of life as a rich and satisfying round of spring lettuce, summer tomatoes, walks in the autumn woods to gather hickory nuts, and popcorn-fireplace winters when, outside, sudden mounds of snow slip from the loaded spruce boughs. All of this was true enough. But they didn't say how, after a morning spent grubbing happily among the pea vines with a scuffle hoe, you come in to find the breakfast dishes still sitting there with the egg congealed, and on your way to collect them you step on an orange crayon.

The country seemed, in my reading, to preclude housekeeping altogether. I would be a kind of para-farmer, but with plenty of time left from country pursuits to sit on a stream bank and enrich my soul with contemplation.

Unhinged with hope, I drove toward the cornfields to meet with a real estate man.

Eventually we meet quite a lot of real estate men. Sooner or later, looking at Emily, they all say cunningly, "And the little girl could have a pony." This dream pony follows us around Chester County on printless hoofs, nuzzling our pockets for sugar, and at night when Emily is asleep you can almost hear it stamp and whinny in her room.

A pony for the little girl. A stream for the little boy twins, underfoot and whining to carry home treasure, a dead branch or a Baggie full of real mud.

Back in town on Sunday nights, I stand in front of the

washing machine emptying pockets. Leaves in Emily's. Stones in the boys', or a mashed grasshopper. No caterpillars, no toads; those have to be left behind with their loving families, although the elaborate little toads are particularly entrancing, and look as if they'd been hand-carved by old Bavarians to hang on a Christmas tree. Very small speckled fish caught in a paper cup have to be dumped back in the stream to rejoin their mommies and daddies. Perfect little red salamanders, like something from Tiffany's, wouldn't be happy in our alley; put them back. On Sunday evenings all our temporary captives stagger groggily back to their families with tales to tell.

All the land we look at seems to us breathtakingly beautiful. We have lived in the city a long time. Every road we drive down, every barn we pass, every tractor, even a bale of hay fallen from a truck and lying sodden in a ditch, makes us catch our breath with incredulous delight. Once we passed some pigs. My husband slammed on the brakes, and we all poured out of the car to run and lean on the fence and look. There were half a dozen of them, yellowish-white patched with mud, snuffling and rooting in a boggy place. They paid no attention to us. We watched them for a long time, and nudged each other with appreciation when one of them lay down to roll in the mud. We smiled and smiled at them, enchanted, all of us. Real pigs. Oh, we had passed cows, hundreds of cows, but there's something not quite authentically countrified about a cow. They might even be fake cows, propped up in a field by some tourist bureau. Pigs were real. No tourist bureau would be capable of falsifying a pig.

We are so easily delighted in our travels that we buy almost everything we look at.

Wyebrook is first. We are never quite virgins again after Wyebrook. Not that we never fall in love again, but our future loves are tinged with caution.

Part of an old estate, it was never farmed, so the poplars and hickories and beeches stand enormous against the sky or, dead, lie massively rotting back into the earth again. (I am pleased with them for doing that, stuffed as I am with *Organic Gardening* and the virtues of humus, and I almost pat the dead trees on the head for their enlightened decomposition.)

The main house of the estate, at the top of the road, is a fairy tale castle with sugarplum turrets, in the most touchingly dreadful taste. An institution now, it is full of mournful children that march in and out, led by nuns. The dry-stone walls of the estate run everywhere, along all the roads. Our land lies just beyond the gateposts. You climb over the low wall and drop steeply down a bank to a stream, hidden from the road. We clear a little glade for picnics, and we come every weekend. The twins go paddling naked and Emily builds stone dams that wash away in the rain. Pheasants whistle crossly at us. Hickory nuts plop down through the leaves.

There's no house here, but this is a minor drawback; we'll just build one, that's all. We send away for a lot of folders of houses that, apparently, someone just brings on a truck and sets up for you.

The house takes on various shapes, like a cloud, but will definitely stand on the old cinder cart-road up the hill. Every evening we take out the dog-eared folders and spread the pictures out on the floor and study them, the size of the bedrooms, the shapes of the decks. They aren't quite what I had had in mind; they don't look much like my crooked old farmhouse with owls; but I concentrate on the thought of trees instead, and the stream.

We narrow the pictures down to three, and finally to one, with lots of glass and a deck all around. Here we will spend our weekends, and our summer vacations, and Christmas, and eventually our retirement. The trees lean down over our imaginary house, green all summer, gold all fall, and the children go sledding down the hill on future snows. Just a bike-ride away the dream pony settles down at a promising-looking farm that seems to have plenty of room; he runs to the fence for sugar when we come around the bend on our bikes in future mornings.

On the practical side, we learn about perc-tests, a process whereby a man digs holes in your land and fills them with water, and then comes around the next day to see if the water's still there. If it is, you can't build a house, or, presumably, you can build a house but can't flush the toilets.

In October, we sit at the place appointed for settlement. We sit for an hour, waiting for our real estate man. He never comes. It turns out, upon investigation, that the land was somehow not his to sell, or anyone else's either, since some legal knot had been tied in its tail, all completely mysterious to us.

The only thing we understand clearly is that we aren't

getting our deposit back, and the real estate man's phone is no longer in service.

The holes for the perc-test are still there, full of leaves, and the dream pony is still waiting at the farm around behind the woods.

It is hard to believe, and impossible to explain to the children. To ward off despair, we drive west again and look some more.

On our old creased, greasy, splotched, tear-stained map of Chester County you can follow our wanderings. The crayon trail to Wycbrook. The cross near Coatesville; that's Sugarman Road, and not easy to find, even with a local map.

Sugarman Road was an enormous stone farmhouse, built in a series of sections and afterthoughts and inspirations over two and a half centuries and full of strange surprising rooms tucked in behind other rooms, fireplaces you could park a Buick in, hulking beams, smells of ancient mold and ten thousand generations of mice. It was as far as you could get in one jump from Wycbrook's prefab vacation house with redwood deck. Even my husband, who is partial to a nice redwood deck, was impressed. The back of the house lay flat against the gravel road, secretly, and you had to walk clear through the house to see what was in front, the terraced gardens, meadow, pond, stream, and woods. It was falling apart, which was why we could afford it, but what difference did that make, what difference did it make that you had to walk through the only bathroom to get at the master bedroom, when there was a tiny boat on the pond and blueberries and pears and crabapples, and a barn for the pony? Some of the other rooms could be made into bathrooms. Heaven knows there were plenty of rooms.

We sign the agreement of sale at once, and I bring out fifty daffodil bulbs and plant them along the terrace steps. Our friends sit in the grass drinking whiskey sours from a thermos and watching Emily ride the dream pony across the sweep of meadow. She switches her legs with a stick and tosses her braids and whinnies.

"It was meant to be," we all assure each other. "We were fated to lose Wyebrook, because this was waiting for us."

"It'll be a showplace," our friends agree. "The *Times* will send photographers. After you get it fixed up a bit, of course," they add, looking up at the porch, which threatens to come loose from the house and rumble down onto our heads.

We never do find out what goes wrong this time. This real estate man apparently sold it to some other people too, and the owners accepted their agreement of sale rather than ours. Why? Was the other buyer richer? Smarter, handsomer, younger, older? We never find out.

We do get our deposit back, though.

The following spring we drive by there, peering wistfully. The new owner has cut down the bushes between the house and the barn, exposing the terraces and meadow to the road. I can't tell whether the daffodils bloomed or not.

By January we feel strong enough to look again. There's the mark on the map, way over by the Lancaster County line. That's Honey Brook. More woods, high on a hill this time, looking out over seven Amish farms with their seven windmills, and little girls in Amish bonnets, and farm ponds shining like coins, and four mules pulling a harrow, and elegant worldly horses pacing in front of their coffin-shaped buggies, harness glittering, nostrils wide. From inside the buggies the bearded Amish regard us disapprovingly.

"It feels like a tourist trap," says my husband. "We'll have to put one of those telescope things on the deck: '10¢ —See the Amish—10¢.'"

But the air is giddy with purity and faint whiffs of pig, and as spring begins to come on early this year lady's-slippers and wild columbine bloom in our woods. Our new woods.

A year has passed. Last spring Wyebrook was white with bloodroot and hepatica and rich with juicy skunk cabbage. The twins are four now, and can walk in the woods without falling down more than every twenty feet. The dream pony is looking a little dingy, the way dreams get, and has developed a shadow: Ben wants one too.

We put a deposit on the Honey Brook hill and get out our tattered pictures of houses. Naturally the price has gone up in leaps of thousands since last spring. And of course the price wasn't quite the whole story, ever; there's the road to cut through the woods to the part with the view, and there's the septic field, and the well.

Kneeling on the floor among our pictures, it occurs to us that we can't afford a second house, not this kind of second house.

We should have thought of it before.

All I had really wanted was a place to take my shoes off on Friday evenings, and to grow tomatoes. It seemed like a simple request. Outrageous for it to cost so much money, when I didn't even *care* if it had bedrooms and bathrooms.

It develops, however, what I might have noticed all along, that the house in my husband's mind never did look much like the house in mine. In my husband's house are many bathrooms. He's deadly serious about bathrooms; there have to be plenty of them, with at least one private to the master bedroom, and they have to be spacious and comfortable and bright with modern appointments. My husband is also sociable, and in his house there were parties, and sliding doors to a deck, and dozens of friends milling around with drinks admiring the view, and spending the night.

We couldn't afford it, not and keep the house we had. On the other hand, it would be rather lonesome for me to buy the shack in *my* mind, since my husband would have to keep driving back to town to shower.

If we went all the way, and sold the house in town, we could afford a house in the country that had bathrooms.

We could commute.

Or I could quit work and my husband could commute.

Our dream fell apart, and clumsily began to reassemble itself in different shapes.

If either of us was going to commute, Honey Brook was simply too far from town, so we said good-by to the seven Amish windmills and the lady's-slippers and our deposit on the land, and made some shorter crayon trips on the map.

There's an arrow there, pointing north toward Coventryville. That house was small, and built of stone before the Revolution, and even before we'd pulled the car off the road I knew that this was it. This was the house I was born to live in. It was a pure and honest shape that seemed to be the correct shape of the human home, the way there's a proper shape for an oriole's nest, and one for a robin's. Any different proportions, size of window, pitch of roof line, seemed distorted after these.

My husband could see at once, from outside, that there would be only one bathroom, and that one quite unsatisfactory, probably cobbled together out of a child's bedroom, with plaster walls and wooden floor. There was almost certainly no room to add another.

We had no key. On tiptoe we peered in the windows at the shapely dusty rooms. Outside there were enormous lilacs blooming, and an apple tree older than God, and a hole down to a root cellar in back, wading in wild daylilies. Best of all, French Creek was the back boundary. French Creek is a young river here, with fish in it, wide enough to have an island, and the island just big enough for children to pitch a tent and sleep among the running waters.

I had to have that house. We could build on a bathroom wing, maybe. The idea of the house grew, and took on the force of some ultimate solace for the accumulating griefs and losses of life. It would open its door and take me in. It would forgive me my sins, and stall the awful passage of time, and always keep me company.

It took me days of tears and sulks to persuade my husband that we might at least call the real estate agent, and get the key, and see inside, although I hardly needed to. I knew my true love when I saw it.

The real estate agent said the house was already sold.

(Memo to whoever bought the house in Coventry Township: When you hear footsteps, or smell that someone's carrying lilacs in, or making applesauce in the middle of the night, don't be alarmed. It's only me.)

For years now, parts of me have gone on living in all the places we were going to live in. I go sledding down the hill at Wyebrook, and pick blueberries and daffodils on Sugarman Road, and watch the windmills turning at Honey Brook. It's rather a confusing way to live, with bits of you broken off and carrying on independently like that.

The house we finally did buy and move into was something of an anticlimax; we staggered into it out of sheer exhaustion. It would need another bathroom, of course, but it did have a stream, and woods. The woods were the special part. The land, sloping and full of rock slides and surprising swampy bits, was plainly no use agriculturally, so the trees, undisturbed, were pioneer trees, pre-Columbian trees, tulip poplars a hundred feet high, beeches three people couldn't reach around, oaks as big as cities, hickories that threw nuts at you, and an underfringe of dogwood, spice bush, and sassafras to chew.

We bought the trees, and the house that went with them.

Privately, on little cat feet, my life went around a corner, but I didn't notice for a while.

I had never really thought of quitting work. I had always worked, and I took it for granted, and I certainly didn't have it in mind to retire. All I really wanted was a place to go barefoot in the summer, and nobody explained that you had to be a housewife to go barefoot, so the whole thing came as a series of interlocking surprises, the way things do in women's lives.

With so many small children, it was obviously dangerous and impractical for me to commute to town. It was just too long a road to be at the other end of when the school nurse called to say they'd broken a leg or come out in spots.

Maybe, once we got established, I could look for a job out there. If I had time. My head was still so full of my reading that I dimly imagined the days crowded with milking goats and getting the hay in before the rain. It is very hard to know, for a woman, just what the different rooms of your life are going to look like till you're in them, and then it's too late.

CHAPTER SEVEN

I take Boy out of his carrying case and set him
down on the grass.

"Maybe he'll get lost," says my husband hopefully. "Or run away."

Boy does not stare around at the grass and trees; it is
not dignified to appear astonished, or even much interested. He sits down and washes, smoothing the smooth fur.
The sun strikes steel-blue glints from its surface.

"Come on," I say. "Come see the woods." He follows
me down the path in the black shade of big trees, placing
his small oval feet delicately in front of each other. He
finds the woods offensively unfamiliar, but if I am here,
then he will be here too. When I get too far ahead he
calls me, and I stop so he can catch up. We move slowly.
Exasperated, I try to pick him up and carry him, but he
struggles to get down. It is not dignified to be carried. We
continue down the path the way we were, Boy just behind
me. We explore our new world slowly, because he will not
trot to keep up. It is not dignified to hurry.

FOR A PRECARIOUS WHILE WE HAVE TWO HOUSES, AND live like kings with a place in the country for weekends, just as we had planned. We furnish the new house with folding cots and empty cartons and insanely ugly lamps from people's attics, and every Friday we pack the family in the car, and a bag of groceries, and drive into the setting sun.

When you have two houses, and plan to go on having two houses, then I suppose you just go out and buy another one of everything: toothbrush, address book, washing machine, nutmeg, soy sauce, calendar, deodorant, television set, Kaopectate, etc. If you are only perched temporarily in this position while you juggle imaginary money from bank to bank, you keep carrying things back and forth. Or back *or* forth. It's not possible to remember which direction any given item went the last time you carried it, so whenever you go to get the cough medicine, or Matthew's boots, or your library book, it's always in the house you aren't in.

Carefully, suspiciously, peeking from under our eyelashes, as it were, we inspect what will be our new neighborhood. There are half a dozen houses strung along the mile of our lane in the woods, presumably with people in them. We aren't sure yet what sort of people. My husband feels suddenly Jewish, something he hadn't noticed in town.

Coming in from an exploratory trip, he reports, "There's a mailbox down the road that says 'Berg.'"

"German," I say nastily. "All the Jewish names out here are German."

"Oh."

"Cheer up. You can be the Jew on the corner. Everyone will feel very liberal and cosmopolitan, as long as there's only one of you. They'll invite you to dinner, and tell everybody afterward that you're really quite nice. Brotherhood Week they'll come over for coffee. No; chicken soup."

He gives me a dark Semitic look and goes to lie down with the *Times*. The very first Sunday after we made settlement, he went out to find a place to buy the Sunday *Times*, and signed up to get it regularly. He carries pieces of it around with him, defiantly, like Matthew with his blanket. He doesn't quite suck his thumb while sniffing its distinctive inky smell, or, if he does, he does it privately, during those long hours in the bathroom.

We both feel a little displaced, and not quite gentlemanly, and slightly hostile from culture shock. Finding out about basseting doesn't help any.

Basseting, it turns out, is the most gentlemanly of the local gentlemanly occupations. They even give a Basset Ball, to which I have never been invited but the mental picture I have of it, given the structural unsuitability of bassets for dancing, is unsettling.

Some people get a gun and go out and shoot a deer, and bring it home, and peel and cook and eat it, but this is not gentlemanly because it has an end in view: food. Some people get on a horse that's chasing a lot of dogs that are chasing a fox, or a stray cat, and this is more gentlemanly because you don't *eat* the fox, or cat. It's also chic on account of the astonishing sums of money you have spent, and everyone knows you have spent, on the horse and all those fancy clothes. The slightly-less-gentlemanly element is that sometimes the hounds really do catch up with whatever they were chasing; even if you don't eat it, it does give the whole thing a certain minimal point: hounds chase something—hounds catch something.

The utterly gentlemanly thing about basseting is that nobody catches anything but maybe a heavy cold.

Basseting is full of aristocratic built-in handicaps designed to make it impossible. One is that bassets, who are supposed to chase rabbits, have been selectively bred so they can't move at all in woods, which are where rabbits live. A basset has to detour around any rock or fallen branch more than four inches high. Bassets are built for sidewalk use, but you can't teach a rabbit to run down a sidewalk. You can't teach a rabbit anything.

Another gentlemanly ingredient is the basset's basic indifference to rabbits. A basset would rather chase a stick than a rabbit, and nothing rather than a stick, a reasonable attitude in a hefty animal with short legs.

The first of our neighbors to speak to us stopped his car where I was dragging some rhododendrons around by the hair, and my husband was watching with his hands in his pockets. (My husband doesn't like helping with outdoor jobs because he says you never know what might be poison ivy. I say *I* know what might be poison ivy and would be glad to tell him, but he seems to think I'm bluffing.)

The neighbor, from his voice, was either a gentleman,

or English, or terribly affected. He introduced himself, and said that the bassets would be at his place at three o'clock, and he certainly hoped we would come.

My husband blinked, and said he didn't think we'd had the pleasure of meeting the Bassets.

The neighbor explained that these were four-legged, small-b bassets, meeting for a hunt, and my husband mumbled something about being a little Jewish boy from Hazleton and went back up to bed with the *Times*.

The children and I kept on moving rhododendrons, and I kept on telling Matthew that trees never, never fell down on people, not even very tall trees like ours. Shortly after three, we were alarmed by a peculiar noise in the woods, like quite a lot of trucks going over a corduroy road in low. The twins clutched me. "Is it *bears?*" whispered Ben.

It was bassets. We went down to see. Our woods were simply creeping with them, bassets stumbling around in circles and climbing over sticks and twigs and oofing at nothing. Milling around mixed in with them were people on foot, and a straggle of children. If the bassets had come to our woods looking for something, they'd forgotten what it was, and drifted around, ears trailing, with no more purpose in life than so many commuters stranded by a sudden strike.

I made the mistake of bending down to pat one. It dropped any lingering thought of rabbits, said "Oof!" in a voice that made the ground shake, and tried to lick my face and had to settle for my knees. Others joined it. I toppled over and vanished under a lurch of bassets, all

anxious for pats and kisses and a spot of intelligent conversation, after that nitwit wading around after rabbits.

The foot traffic that had come with them stood around
looking dissatisfied. The heaviest basset sat down on me,
and the rest leaned against me; several went to sleep.

A sturdy woman in army boots blew on a Boy Scout
bugle, which roused the people but not my new friends.
Some of the more businesslike humans began to plow off
toward the northwest; our fence got in their way for a
while, but not for long. The posts were probably rotten
anyway, and toppled easily. In hot pursuit of the humans
streamed the pack of small children, baying on the scent.
A basset licked my ear.

The bugle sounded again, a stirring call to action,
and Emily danced with impatience. "Come *on*," she cried.
"They're leaving, come on, let's *go*."

I pulled myself out from under the heap, and the children and I trotted away down the path after the hunt,
across our flattened fence. Reluctantly the bassets, rather
than be left with no one to talk to, arose (or seemed to;
it's hard to tell with bassets) and wallowed after us.

Away went the hunt. First the hunters, crashing through
the trackless forest, then the local children, quarreling
and pushing each other into the stream, then me and
my children. Then the bassets, some of whom we had to
lift across the stream, ten inches deep in its profoundest
pools. It's possible that far in front of us all, in front
even of the lady with the bugle, was a rabbit, although
probably it was just a vision of dry socks and martinis.
I prefer to think the rabbit was bringing up the rear,

loping easily along somewhere back beyond the remotest basset.

We didn't last long. Thick, prickery woods are tough enough even without a child clutching each arm. "Is this the *wild woods?*" hissed Matthew.

I told him no, it was just a plain woods. He looked unconvinced.

"I heard a bear," said Ben. "This time it really was a bear."

We turned back, in what I cheerfully insisted was the direction of home, but Emily went on with the hunt, and got lost, and came home after dark, scratched and muddy. Several bassets turned back with us. One sat down to bite its fleas, and another was trying to lift its leg at a tree and kept losing its balance. The rest had disappeared. Gone home, no doubt, where they were sitting in front of a jolly fire telling lies about rabbits. A light chilly drizzle misted the air. Far, far away the bugle sounded again.

We find our way home with only a minimum of panic from the twins and phony confidence from me, and I make myself a stiff scotch, feeling very gentlemanly, very Chester County. Very superior to my husband, sleeping upstairs with his cheek on the crossword puzzle while *I* have been out hunting.

Later he comes downstairs carrying the Travel Section and looks moodily out the window for a while. "Wait till we move, and I start commuting," he says. "They'll have to put a separate car on the Paoli express. Marked '*Juden.*' "

THE SECOND NEIGHBOR I MEET IS A HOUSEWIFE.

She comes to call dressed in an apricot-colored poly-
ester pants suit. I try to choose her a place to sit from
among our collection of boxes and broken chairs, and
notice for the first time what a lot of mud has stuck to the
floor. There's a lot on me, too. I've been digging young
hemlocks out of what's going to be a flower bed.

She welcomes me to the neighborhood. I thank her
shyly, and offer to warm up some coffee. She accepts. I
find that I am babbling and falling over my own furniture,
and realize I am afraid of housewives. They make me feel
awkward and self-conscious, and I swerve hysterically between childish prattle and hostile silence, gripped by the
kind of social panic that seizes one in the presence of the
terminally ill. What do you *say* to a housewife? Let a
woman tell me that she spends at least some of her time
as a sculptor or a postal clerk or a chemist, and we're old
buddies in no time, but I can as easily talk to Eskimos as
housewives. I giggle, and spill the coffee.

She is formal but cordial. The neighborhood, she tells
me, is real friendly. They all take their mending over to
Sally Ansell's family room, and I can come too, and we
can all mend together.

The prospect fills me with terror. I would sooner be
boiled in oil. Also, how to explain that I have no mending?
I never mend. When a button comes off something, I put
the button in a safe place and lay the garment across the
back of a chair, so I won't forget. When there are enough
things piled on the chair to be inconvenient, I throw them
away. They're probably outgrown by then, and anyway

most of them were free to begin with. My children have cousins, and the cousins are pretty hard on their clothes but if they're still recognizable as clothes my children wear them. Besides, there's a thrift shop on my regular route to work, where, if you hit it the right day, you can buy a shopping bag full of children's shirts for a dollar.

So I joyfully accept the invitation to mend at Sally Ansell's, knowing I will spend the rest of my life trying to weasel out of it. Hiding under the bed, and telling lies about my mending.

Actually, I did darn a sock for my husband once, when we were freshly married, but he wouldn't wear it.

Now, are the people who mend at Sally Ansell's the same people who go basseting? The same people who ride to hounds? No, they can't be; more likely the wives of the people who shoot deer. Women go basseting, women go fox hunting, but the deer hunters' wives stay home and mend. I can see that things are more complicated here than I had thought, me with my simple-minded vision of us all working in the fields together singing. Where are we going to fit in here? And how will anyone know where we fit in, since my husband's hunting is limited to rolled newspapers and mosquitoes?

I am confused, and continue confused for a long time, until eventually the business with the pony clears it up.

CHILDREN FROM THE AREA APPEAR, AFOOT AND ON BIKES, and lurk along the road peering through the trees at us. After the first few weekends, they apparently decide we are harmless and start throwing rocks at our kids. Emily throws rocks back.

THE SMALL-GAME SEASON MAKES THE WOODS HIDEOUS with shotgun fire. Matt and Ben, who watch too much television, refuse to leave the shelter of the house, and cannot be convinced that no one is firing at *them*. I am not very convinced myself. Some of the shooting is quite close by, and in the woods across the lane I see small groups of hunters moving purposefully through the underbrush, with guns. They are close enough so that I can hear sticks snap under their boots, and from time to time they shoot.

At one point I am out dredging up some laurel, and I straighten up and holler toward them, "Hey, you can't hunt there! That land's all posted."

No answer.

"Can't you read the signs? Besides, you're too close to the house. I've got kids playing in the woods." (A lie: they're huddled over the television.)

No answer, but a single, ear-shattering shot. Twigs shower down on me where I am standing, and some oak leaves. He has fired into the tree over my head. A gentle warning: housewives armed only with a spade should speak civilly to men with guns.

Chastened, I go back in the house and curl up with one of my books about moving to the country.

WE GO DOWN THE LANE AND CUT A CHRISTMAS TREE AND bring it home, and all agree that it smells better than city-boughten trees.

Winter in the country is different from winter in the city. It's more comfortable, because you don't have to do all that walking around and waiting for cabs and buses, but it is also much colder; we gather respectfully around the thermometer the day it gets down to ten below. I build huge reckless extravagant fires of our own free wood, in front of which I thaw the boots and mittens. It snows, and I buy a sled. All day long Ben sleds down and trudges up the path, caked with several inches of frozen snow. Ben is one of those children who can't get within three feet of any malleable substance, jelly, mud, snow, or chicken grease, without acquiring an even coat of it everywhere, even behind the ears. (Kids like this were considered amusing back when people had maids, and a laundress.) Now there is as much snow in his hair as on his boots. My husband, who has never accepted the germ theory and holds that all illness is a punishment for wrong living, predicts that he will get flu. Irritatingly, he does. We all do.

CHAPTER EIGHT

We have to sell our house in town.

In our arrogance and innocence we decide to sell it ourselves. Who knows it as well as we? We alone know which things they'd better not look at, like the laundry room, where the washer and drier were installed before the kitchen wall was up, and the doorway's too small, and when the washer and/or drier breaks down (they've been making funny noises lately, too) the wall will have to be dynamited in order to get them out and new ones in. When the furnace breaks down, two walls will have to be dynamited.

We paint everything except the window glass. Before painting the third-floor hall, I get a measuring tape and pencil and paper, and carefully record the dated height marks from the boys' doorframe, including those of visiting cousins. I fold the paper carefully and put it in my wallet, to be reproduced on a doorframe at the new house. Armed with this essential information, I feel ready to move.

I spend a fortune on hothouse daisies, lay a couple of

classy magazines on the coffee table, and stand back and squint. Really, it looks nice. All dressed up like a pig at a party; if I didn't know it so well I'd buy it myself.

The outside of the house doesn't look quite so civilized. I can see how our alley mightn't seem as homey to strangers as it does to me. Directly in front of our door someone has dropped a bunch of celery, and snow has melted and frozen again until now the celery is securely preserved under two inches of dirty ice. It seems to be in pretty fair condition still; almost fit to eat; but to the prospective house-buyer it just might look like garbage.

We put an ad in the paper, and on Sundays we show people around.

Most of our serious customers are men, pairs of quietly housekeeping bachelors; women don't like the neighborhood: there are blacks as well as celery. Not respectable, upwardly mobile blacks, either. Poor blacks, immobile. At one end of our alley another, even smaller alley intersects it, and its crooked little brick houses shelter quite a lot of them. Our customers flatly refuse to believe that they have been pleasant and peaceable neighbors to us for six years. They don't even like the Cat Lady. We can't very well hide her; there she stands at the corner where she always stands, looking like something in black granite, arms folded, at her feet the mother of our cat Betsey, and a whiskery little dog, and assorted foundlings. If St. Francis had been a stout black lady advanced in years he would have looked like that.

Does she look sinister to our prospective customers? You bet.

My black neighbors sit out front in the sun on pleasant days, and return my children when they wander, and
when we meet in the mornings, smile, and observe that it
sure did rain last night, didn't it.

I find myself bristling and overdefending the place to
our customers. This is my home: how dare they think it's
dangerous? We won't sell it to them. They can't have it.
I'll stay. Yes, I know (Mrs. Coleman, is it?), I've noticed
the two empty houses down there, boarded up, and the
alley cats slinking in and out. (And that ain't all, either;
we got rats as big as collies, folks keep 'em for watchdogs.
Train 'em to pull a cart.) Yes, I've seen the graffiti, and the
old board fence buckling under its vines. This is *my* alley
you're sneering at, madam, and if I could paint I would
never paint anything else, I would paint a thousand pictures of all those brick planes intersecting, and ailanthus
trees and cats, and roofs and chimneys: go away. You can't
have my house.

These are my three children, they don't come with the
house, ha ha ha. (See, they're still alive, scarcely scarred,
barely maimed. That whiny little Joel of yours in the fur
coat; do him good to live here. Kathy Passyn'll wipe up
the street with him.)

The living room is nineteen feet by sixteen. These doors
go out to the balcony. That's the balcony. The fireplace
works very well. If you can afford the wood, ha ha. (For
our first Sunday of showing, I had laid a lovely fire, and
when the first customers rang the doorbell I lit it, and
ran to open the door. Behind me great churning choking
billows of smoke poured out of the fireplace and up the

open staircase, and filled every room in the house so that we staggered around with hankies over our noses like firemen; I had forgotten to open the flue.)

I straighten a chair. This is the study, we have a couch in it that opens into a double bed, or you could use it for a fourth bedroom.

At least my husband isn't here. I get sick enough of my own voice without hearing his too, on another floor, saying the same words I just said ("And this is the children's bathroom, and here is the linen closet") through my own voice saying what he just finished saying ("We made the bookshelves to fit in that alcove, so of course they go with the house").

These people today (Finch? No, they were last week. Finister?) look in silence, suspiciously. I prefer the ones who talk, and ask questions. The silent ones drive me into an endless monologue full of wobbly little jokes, which they absorb into blank faces.

I have arranged a pitcher and a pretty casserole on top of the refrigerator. This annoys Boy, who normally sits there, but hides the fact that the cupboards above it slant downhill. Everything in the house slants, but these cupboards are especially precipitous. Am I a born salesman, then, a natural liar? No, I think it's more like sending a child to a party. I want people to like the house, to think it's pretty, more than I want them to buy it. Old corduroys, so to speak, are okay for just the family, but to hold it up in front of the world I want its floors waxed and daisies on the table; look, see my pretty child.

These people today are lock-testers, and inspect the

doors and windows. We get lock-testers, space-and-size nuts with measuring tapes, appliance freaks, carpentry fanatics, and people who want to know what's inside the walls and floors. (*Inside* them? Dunno. Lost marbles, beads, toast crusts, pennies, cat hairs? Treasure? Dragons bleached albino from their long years in the dark? Emily's library card?)

The doorbell rings and I excuse myself and hurry down to answer it, putting on my customer smile as I go. Please, God, don't let it be Derek. I open the door with a jerk, to minimize the groan it gives when opened slowly. It's Derek.

We look at each other for a while, and I think about a lot of things.

Matt and Ben are in private all-day nursery school because I work, and Emily is in a private grade school because she seemed so little and vulnerable for our fierce public one. The cost is astonishing. ("That can't be the bill," says my husband hopefully. "Maybe it's their phone number.") Each class contains six or eight black children, all cleaner, politer, and better-dressed than my own, and probably smarter, too, since most of them are on scholarship. You'd have to be positively potty with bigotry to object to them coming over to play.

Black Derek, however, is something else. Derek's speech is mysterious, his games are rough, and a complicated musty smell arises from his unwashed clothes. He lives somewhere around. Sometimes he brings a brother. I assume he has a home, and more family; I never asked. Derek is a cheerful, independent fellow, not a fit subject for sympathetic prying. Even Emily the snob likes Derek, and the twins adore him. He is the only eight-year-old with time for them. It is Derek who brings back abandoned balls and tricycles before they get stolen or crunched by cars, and even drags home from time to time a heavy, screaming, bleeding twin. He's been coming around for a couple of years now; when he leaves, I go through the house with a sponge and wipe off the perfect five-pointed black handprints from the walls. My husband says, "Couldn't you just ask him to wash his hands when he comes to play? Politely, of course?" Well, I've been thinking about it, but I haven't yet.

So there he stands, Derek the dirty, son of the slums, on the doorstep, and he wants to come in and play.

It's no problem, really. I just have to say, "Not today, Derek," and close the door. He will not be hurt or insulted; he will go to the neighbors' and play there. I do not need Derek today. I stand and struggle with inertia, honesty, defiance, cowardice, and various other things.

"Benjamin home?" he asks, finally.

"Sure," I say. "They're in their room. Go on up." (And stay there. Keep the *door* closed.)

My customers are muttering together in the study. With luck, I can get them through the house and out without encounters.

They want to see the kitchen again. They open and close the oven door a lot, frowning. Then the study again. These are serious lookers, seriously interested, not just killing a Sunday afternoon. We go back up to the bedrooms, and they test the window latches. We go into the twins' room, but mysteriously there is no one there.

Besides, one of the window latches is broken, three flights above the street. I have a mental picture of burglars being lowered on a string by accomplices from the roof. Spiderman, maybe. Stung, I say, "This is really a very quiet neighborhood. We've never had any trouble." They don't bother to answer. They know what they know.

And so back to the living room, and of course that's where the missing children are. Emily and Matthew are watching television. Derek, kind Derek, is making something with string for Benjamin. Ben wrestles with him, climbing on his back. "Get offa me, now quit," says Derek shrugging. Ben rolls off. The room has developed a complicated musty smell.

My customers have too much self-control to look at each other, but their eyes slide around sideways to meet at the corners.

I feel suddenly quite cheerful as I take them to the door. "Well, thank you," they say. "We'll have to think it over. We'll call you . . ."

Oh no, you won't. Back to the suburbs with you, back to Radnor, back to Meadowbrook, good-by, good-by. "Watch your step," I say, maliciously a moment too late. "We have quite a problem here. Dogs, you know." And they leave, walking quickly and trying to scrape their shoes clean as they go.

I stand awhile on the doorstep. It's nice, in March, to have a little dusk, after the sudden winter nights. Nice to see that spring kind of softness in the light as it hangs

on. The celery is gone. The church bells start to ring six
o'clock. Joe the Greek, who owns the junk store on the
corner, comes swinging down the alley. "Nice evening,"
he says.

"Almost spring," I agree.

The church bells ring a flat, iron note, ba-ang, ba-
ang. The dampness in the air makes them harsher, and
even more flatted; you can almost taste the iron in their
voice, and this has come to be the authentic sound of
spring to me, the way tires swishing in the wet on Lombard Street mean fall. Ba-ang, ba-ang, ba-ang. They don't
seem meant to be music at all, but just there to tell me
where I am and what time it is, otherwise how would I
ever know?

I can feel the tears of pure homesickness rising behind
my nose, and go inside and slam the door viciously.

PEOPLE COME, AND STAY AND HAVE A DRINK WITH US
and talk, or go away, and come back to look again and
bring someone. They're always bringing someone else,
nobody can make up his own mind about where to live.
They bring their mothers, their sisters-in-law, their best
friends, their *dentists,* for heaven's sake, but nobody has
the sense, thank God, to bring in anyone like a carpenter,
or an electrician, or anyone who's going to notice there's
no beam under the fireplace, and whoever sits at that end
of the dining room, underneath it, is apt to be wearing
a lot of bricks around the head and shoulders, one of
these days.

The crowd thins out to a few people who come back

again and again. It narrows down to a pair of bachelors, whom we like, and the Macmillans, whom we don't.

Lots of people love the house but wouldn't dream of buying it. The Macmillans seem to hate it, but want to buy it. Or else they just pretend to hate it, for fear we'll raise the price if they smile. All one can say for them is that they are city folk, and not startled by blacks. They come again and again and again, and eventually notice everything, like how the sliding closet doors fall on your head if opened hastily. They sneer at the slanting cupboards.

One evening they appear while my husband and I are cooking, and we send them off on their own to poke and disapprove. We are sick of Macmillans, and we don't care what they find out, like how the ventilating fans in the bathroom just go round and round and aren't vented anywhere. At least they aren't likely to find out that the overflow pipe from the children's bathtub feeds into the living room ceiling. Not unless it occurs to them to look at the ceiling. Or take a bath.

Mrs. Macmillan has one of those enormous embroidered woolen pocketbooks people buy in Peru or somewhere, and she leaves it on the dining room couch. Boy walks slowly over to the couch, and jumps up on it, and sits looking at the pocketbook for a long time. It is hard to guess what's going on in his mind; he seems hypnotized.

Then, swiftly, before we can shout, he pees on it. All over it. A veritable lake of pee, all over the pocketbook and trickling onto the couch. Then he leaps tidily down and walks away.

I turn the couch cushion over, and dab at the pocket-book with paper towels, but quite a lot has already soaked in. We do not hit the cat. I almost wish I'd thought of it myself.

The bachelors stop by for a drink and inform us, sadly, that they have bought a house in Radnor instead, with a garden.

It is never recorded what Mrs. Macmillan thinks about her pocketbook. However, they buy our house, and I begin to interview for my replacement at the office.

Quite a lot of people apply for my job, respectable, grown-up, professional people, and I am mildly surprised that they'd be interested. Of course, whoever gets it will be making more money than I am. Five thousand dollars a year more than I am. This information is so unsettling that I really can't think of anything suitable to say to my bosses about it, and end up saying nothing. For them, there's nothing odd about it at all. The new person is not expected to do better work, or more of it; there is only the one copywriter, and only those same old accounts. The new person will simply sit here longer. The new person will show up in the morning and depart in the evening at the same hour as everyone else, instead of slipping frivolously off to bathe her kids and decide whether to broil or fry the chicken for dinner, and whether to have potatoes or rice.

My feelings are hurt. I feel unloved. Nastily, I recommend a person who will certainly hate it there, and they will hate her too, and I clean out my desk without really noticing that this is the end of my career, and go home to pack.

I AM FORCED TO CONFRONT EMILY'S ROOM.

Now, Emily is a pack rat and a Virgo, and I expect her to keep things. I expect her to have a shell collection, a stone collection, a leaf collection, and a pieces-of-wood collection, as well as every drawing she ever drew and every school paper since kindergarten. But there are some things I wasn't expecting. The cello case, for instance, at least I think it's a cello case; I don't know much about these things. It's enormous, and except for being badly scuffed, and one hinge missing, and the latch doesn't work, and the handle's been replaced with string, it's in perfect condition. Some crazy person put it out for the trash, on Pine Street. And why keep every pair of shoes you've owned since you were four, why, why?

"They might come in useful. Some day."

"Useful for what?"

Mulishly she averts her eyes and crouches protectively over the battered curling sandals.

Then there's the horse, an unspeakable plastic horse about seven hands high that used to have wheels, I think, and its head won't stay on and has to sit beside it on the floor. The Passyn children threw it *away,* can you imagine? And then there's this ant farm. There aren't any ants in it, and there never were any ants in it, but there's a lot of dirt and sticks she put in a shirt box two years ago in case she should find some ants. It's labeled on the top, ANT FARM, in case some idiot might think it was just a shirt box full of dirt and sticks. And then there are the usual jigsaw puzzles with two pieces missing, and bald four-year-old cattails, and rumpled peacock feathers from the zoo, and necklaces with no catch and pins with no pins, and posters from school fairs and hand-decorated boxes containing another box containing four jacks and a marble, and rocks as big as your head containing genuine quartz, and paintboxes containing no paint except white, and still I'm only four feet in from the door.

Is it a sickness? Do I send her to a child psychologist? Or just soak it all with kerosene and throw in a match? It seems a little backward for nine. I know nine-year-olds who are *engaged,* and not for the first time, either. Maybe I'd rather have her this way, but I must admit an engagement ring would be easier to pack and move than Emily's collection of the cardboard inner rolls from paper towels.

I bring up some large trash bags and throw away a thousand elderly Christmas cards and some pots of shriveled cacti and the collection of crazed windshield glass from various collisions on Lombard Street. Emily howls, and I reluctantly return one of the finest pieces. It really is rather beautiful.

The dried-mud collection stops me for a minute. "But *why?*"

"It's a good way to store it," she explains. It is molded into smooth careful balls about the size of an orange, and covers the floor under the bed.

"Store it for *what?*"

"In case you need it. Then you just get it wet, and there it is."

Instant mud.

The next day, while she's safely in school, I carry downstairs seven of the largest-size trash bags full of things.

The things I leave behind me mate, and are fruitful and multiply, before I am two flights down.

The boys are easier. All their possessions are broken beyond hope, and I throw out everything but their security blankets and their beds.

In the back of the liquor cabinet I discover a bottle of Courvoisier with about two tablespoonfuls in it, and a bottle of Grand Marnier with nearly a half an inch. They have been there a long time. They are there because it feels better to say, "I can't make that, I don't have enough Grand Marnier," rather than, "I don't have *any* Grand Marnier."

I sit cross-legged on the floor, a bottle in each hand, considering. Do I take them along? Wrap them in towels and *pack* them? That's ridiculous. On the other hand, do I pour them down the sink? *Throw it away?*

I sit for a long time thinking, and then unstopper them and, sitting on the floor at nine thirty-five in the morning, I drink them, first the brandy, then the Grand Marnier, and throw the bottles in the trash.

CLUTCHING AN ARMFUL OF YOWLING CATS, I SLAM THE CAR door and we drive away. I look back, expecting our whole lives in this house to pass before my eyes, like drowning, but all I can remember is the time Emily ate the aspirin, and the time it snowed for our Christmas party and we all ran out on the balcony and gathered it up and pelted snowballs around the living room. Somebody broke a lamp.

Boy howls dismally and scrabbles at the closed windows of the car.

My husband is a compulsive voter. He really loves to vote, and will vote for anyone or anything, even those inscrutable bond issues involving loans to the fire department or draining the marshes beyond the airport. Personally, I can take it or leave it, and waver between believing my vote can't make any possible difference so why bother, and being afraid it just might, conceivably, make some enormous, unforeseen difference and destroy us all.

I go with him anyway, of course, and of course our first step after moving, before we hang the pictures or decide where to put the couch, is to register to vote from our new house.

Registration is held at the junior high school, one of those new flat schools they build in the country, with a view of fields and woods.

A brisk little girl is typing. I stand in line, and then it's my turn.

She rolls in the form, and types my name and address and political party. "Occupation?" she says. "Housewife?"

There is only a minimal question in her voice; she has to ask it, but she knows the answer.

I look wildly around the room for help. My husband is busy with a different brisk little girl. No one else seems to care.

"Wait," I say to the girl.

She looks up. She has already typed as far as the "s."

"Nothing," I say. "Never mind."

"e-w-i-f-e," she types.

So this is where I've been going, all along.

I have a mental picture of a rather dim-witted looking chicken, one of those white ones with little red eyes, head down, following a trail of corn into a drop-gate box.

Part Two

CHAPTER ONE

Five minutes after we arrived in the country it started to rain, and it rained all summer. People looked at us oddly and said they never remembered a summer like that. Somewhere in the middle of the rain was Hurricane Agnes.

We did notice that it was coming down pretty hard, but we were all sick of the house by then, and my husband was persuaded to take us all to Phoenixville for a hamburger at Gino's. We ate our hamburger, and got back in the car. As we drove out of the town, most of it disappeared behind us under the roaring waters of the Schuylkill River, but we didn't hear about that till later. When we got to our own road the bridge over the creek was under quite a lot of fast water. We drove two miles farther to the next bridge, but it seemed to be gone entirely, so we went back to the first. You could still see its ramparts, out in the middle of a lot of creek. The creek was everywhere, with stuff spinning along in it, and made an unpleasantly *heavy* noise compared to its usual light chatter.

My husband said, crossly, that there didn't seem to be any other way to get home and we couldn't just sit there, so we drove through the creek toward the bridge. Matt and Ben crouched on the floor. Emily cheered. We rose up over the crest of the bridge, and down the other side, and floated.

Now, everyone knows VWs float, because they ran all those ads about it, but it never seemed very urgent before. I mean if I want a boat, I'll get a boat. But suddenly there we were, rushing sideways across what used to be a field, and we rocked and swayed in the way nobody expects a car to rock and sway. (Memo to VW: I would like to complain that the twins, on the floor of the back seat, were elbow-deep in water. If we were planning to go very far, we'd have to bail.)

My husband was extremely angry. He is a civilized man, and his idea of a natural disaster is what pigeons do on the seats of park benches. "This was a mistake," he said, but you could tell it wasn't *his* mistake.

He gunned the engine. Presumably the wheels went around. We headed, sideways, for the Schuylkill River, and thence to the Delaware, and the open sea. Kon-Tiki. The twins wept. Uprooted trees swirled around us.

My husband, for lack of anything better to do, continued to gun the engine.

Through no navigational virtue of our own, we hit a piece of rising ground and the wheels caught. Fountains leaped up behind us. Like a Mississippi stern-wheeler we churned our way cross-current over the field, onto land again, and the road, and home, with a nasty lake full of peanut shells and popsicle sticks slopping back and forth on the floor. We parked our car in the driveway, and later, when the repair shop surfaced in the mud and reopened for business, had it towed away and the wiring replaced. (It was pretty gallant of it to take us clear home, not to mention through the raging waters, but that was a gallant car. It never broke down anywhere except in its own driveway, and would be living yet if I hadn't . . . well, never mind. Anyway, I miss it. It had heart. I should have had it stuffed and mounted.)

At some point in the summer the rain stopped being Hurricane Agnes and became just plain rain again, though I don't see how they could tell. The water level on Main Street went down some.

Everything mildewed. My husband and I, as soon as we had registered to vote, painted the entire inside of the house, and now it was covered with creeping black mildew. The tile floor sweated, the furniture waded in water, the rugs mildewed. The baseboards turned green. The upholstery grew fur. The books bent and curled, and dark books sprouted white mildew and light books sprouted black mildew and they all stank. An occasional toadstool popped up under the sink. The piano rotted. I kept washing and wearing the same clothes every day, like Orphan Annie, because none of my bureau drawers would open. All my shoes were too wet and mossy to wear so I went around barefoot on the sloppy floor; my toenails wrinkled.

Once in a while the sun promised to come out, and I carried all the rugs and shoes outside and spread them on the sopping lawn, and then it rained.

Emily signed up for riding lessons at a local stable, where mostly they sat inside and cleaned tack, and learned the names of different kinds of bits, and listened to the rain on the roof and the horses munching gratefully in their stalls.

Down at the general store, it was unanimously agreed that all this monkeying around with space projects had done a lot of damage, and weather hadn't really been the same since the first moon landing.

I stopped bathing. It seemed insane to turn on a tap and get the stuff on purpose.

Whenever it stopped raining for a minute I went out and gardened organically, puttering around with ladybugs and soggy, beastly, underdone compost that still smelled remarkably like garbage. When horses went by on the road and dropped a pile of manure, I scooped it up tenderly and fed it to the garden.

Horses went by often. There were horses all over. Just down the hill was a whole field full of shetlands, cross and shaggy, harboring the morose uncharitable thoughts that occupy a shetland's idle hours. In front of the house, brisker ponies went by, under serious little girls in hard hats. Once when I was squatting down pulling crabgrass out of the lawn, which was dumb, because when I was finished there wasn't any lawn left and the children slithered around in the mud, I got a watched, prickly feeling at the back of the neck, and turned, and there were three ponies standing there looking at me. I smothered a shriek. They were about six feet away, under a cherry tree, watching me with the alert and patient look of an audience waiting for the curtain to go up.

Emily got some string and we tied it around the neck of the largest one, and led it, with the others following, down to the field of morose shetlands, and pushed them in through a broken place in the fence. We didn't know if they belonged there or not, and we still don't, but I doubt if anyone cared. There are plenty of ponies around here. In the beginning I hollered for Emily whenever they went down the lane, and the two of us pressed our noses to the window and gawked at the incredible, astounding sight of actual little girls on horseback riding by. After a while, though, I stopped hollering, and finally stopped noticing at all.

Emily continued to learn the names of bits and save every cent she could get her fingers on. She had forty-two dollars. I began to feel uneasy; in an area where you can't chuck a rock over your shoulder without striking horseflesh, where you can't even pull *crabgrass* without a lot of ponies hanging around staring, forty-two dollars is probably plenty.

The windshield wiper on the driver's side gave up, exhausted. Twice a week I bought a new box of salt and threw away the solid, sweating lump of the old one. None of the doors would close; they still won't; it was a devastating summer. After a particularly heavy downpour a baby pig washed down the road and came to rest in the yard, drowned, with its little front trotters pressed on either side of its nose. A family discussion ensued as to whether we should eat it, ignore it, or bury it, and if the last, whose job *that* was, and if the first, who had to take the necessary preliminary steps. The discussion went on for several days, and presently the pig disappeared.

Benjamin painted empty boxes in the garage, and pounded nails into scrap lumber and left the results in the driveway, pointed end up, and searched for bugs for his pet toad.

Matthew, his spirit unsettled by the move, followed me around at my gardening with his blanket pressed to his nose.

He said, "We could get a cow."

I looked at the confusion of lawn, or lawns, with its steep terraces and stone walls and, beyond that, towering forest. "We don't have a proper place to keep a cow. A cow needs a pasture. There's no room here."

Matthew inhaled his blanket and gazed dreamily into the distance. "It could lie down there," he said, pointing. "In the driveway, it could lie down. I could lie down beside it."

I see them sometimes still, out of the corner of my eye, lying there on the graveled turnaround; skinny Matt, who no matter what he wears always looks tattered, one of nature's waifs, and the cow, a cream-colored one, chewing slowly and staring around her in the mild, unastonished way of cows.

Emily developed a tentative friend from down the lane, and the two of them cantered together across the front lawn, switching their thighs and speaking sternly to them. Sidney got chased up trees. If there was a dog in the township bored and restless, it would stop by to chase Sidney shrieking up a tree, where he continued to scream piercingly for hours after the dog had gone home and we were all standing around the foot of the tree urging him down with baby talk and tuna fish.

Betsey, however, a slum cat from the alleys, took to the woods as if born there, and every morning we found on the front walk, laid out for our approval and possible consumption, an assortment of moles and meadow mice and short-tailed shrews. She caught frogs, and, not being sure what one does with a frog, brought them into the house, meowing interrogatively with her mouth full. Benjamin rescued them. If that's your idea of rescue. Ben preyed on the wildlife. He caught toads. He caught toads as big as your two fists and toads as small as your thumbnail, and carried them around in his warm little hands and lavished them with kisses, and they staged daredevil escapes with the courage born of despair. I tried to keep track, but always had the uneasy feeling that there was one unaccounted for and loose in the house somewhere, crouched under a bureau miserably bulging its throat and waiting to die.

Then there were lightning bugs. Ben brought them in to show me, and opened his fist reverently, and they flew away and the house filled up with them, invisible until bedtime. Always, at the last moment before sleep, I was groggily aware that in the bedroom a lightning bug was circling, circling, signaling frantically to his comrades outside.

Boy spent his nights in bed for the most part, and

his days, when the rain stopped, following me decorously around the garden, along with Matthew.

Matthew said, "I wish we could have another boy."

"You mean," I asked warily, "a *baby?*"

"Yes, and you know what could be its name?"

"What?"

"Its name could be . . . Arnold."

"Where would it sleep?" My mind raced through the bedrooms; there was no room for Arnold. Thank goodness.

"It could sleep here," said Matthew. We both looked down at the narrow slit of space he offered, between the bend of his arm and the shadowed hoops of his ribs. "Inside my arm, it could sleep."

I think about Arnold from time to time. He has joined Emily's dream pony, and follows me around, part of a quiet faithful caravan of ghosts I have picked up over the years, shadowing my garden chores. None of these things seems especially reproachful, but they are *there,* and I wish they would stop it. Arnold, and that damned cow, and a lovely red Doberman bitch named Rasha. A truck was coming at me in the other lane, and she just came swooping from nowhere, like a deer, and there was nothing I could do. Nothing but pull back on the wheel and jam and jam at the brake and brace myself for the thud. She follows me, looking up with hopeful, affectionate eyes the way she did from the snowbank at the side of the road. She was young, not much more than a pup, and you could see she didn't believe it was true.

Benjamin also caught a lot of snakes, but I was

pleased to note that most of them were basically worms, or centipedes. He carried them around and crooned to them.

I found it hard to settle to anything because I kept waiting for the sitter or someone to take the boys off my hands so I could get some work done. Nobody did.

Since I was a housewife, I decided to mop the floor, although it was pretty wet already without my help. Mopping encouraged it. It gleamed like a lake, deeper under the couch and chairs. I kept screaming at the children not to run, it was *slippery,* but Matthew nevertheless slid six feet into the aluminum lip of the sliding door and opened his forehead. Being both housewife and homesteader, I mended it myself, laying him out on the bathroom floor and kneeling in blood and water, trying to press the lips of the wound together long enough to nail them shut with a Band-Aid, and mopping blood with a towel. Frankly, it was a lousy job, and the scar is enormous, but there's nothing a little boy enjoys so much as a good scar.

Exhausted from mopping and surgery, I screamed at them some more not to run, and they ran anyway, and I said no, they couldn't have any cookies or any supper either, because Mommy was tired. My husband came home and coasted into a lamp, and said consolingly that it would probably dry when the weather changed. Sure enough, on Tuesday a high front came through and the floor dried, leaving thousands and thousands of footprints of all sizes, including the cats', which looked rather sweet.

Occupation: ?

EVERY MORNING, I FEEL GUILTY ABOUT NOT GOING TO work, but I'm used to feeling guilty. We all are. I feel guilty about going to work; not going to work; being so tired I scream at the kids; and not having done enough work to be so tired I scream at the kids. Guilt's a chronic condition of housewifery, and compounded by motherhood. Kiss them passionately at bedtime to atone for the sins of the day. Yelling like that about the cookies; heavens, they're only lousy cheap grocery-store cookies (Why don't you make your own? Huh? Something wholesome, with wheat germ; bet all the other mothers do) and surely he can have all he wants. There he was, standing on the stove rummaging in the cupboard for cookies, and you yelled like that; he could have lost his balance and fallen. You *monster.*

The following day you come into the kitchen and he's standing on the stove again, rummaging again for cookies, and apparently never even heard what you said the day before. He's used to it. (Calloused and cynical, no doubt, from the way you scream all the time.) There's probably something else you're doing, something you haven't even thought to feel guilty about, that will ruin his life. Twenty years later, it'll turn up. Here you are losing sleep over the really *awful* things you said to him, the time he put the Silly Putty in the oven, and how he'll never get over it, and then it'll turn out that what he can't get over is what you did to that frog in the washing machine. He's forgotten the oven, and you've forgotten the frog.

ONE OF THE FIRST THINGS I DISCOVER ABOUT NOT GOING
to work any more is that I don't have any money, which
for some reason comes as a shock. Anyone of normal
intelligence would have figured it out in advance: if you
cut the family income nearly in half, you have less money
than before. I suppose it was the way my husband used
to gripe about the taxes that confused me. He was fond
of saying, when I worked, that we couldn't afford what it
did to the taxes; it was costing us a fortune; I would have
to quit and stay home.

He was wrong. After I quit working there wasn't, for
instance, any money at all for clothes. It was several years
before my husband and I were personally affected; after
all, we had clothes already, and simply continued to wear
them till they rotted on our backs. We didn't grow. The
children, on the other hand, were almost instantly naked.
My old friend the thrift shop was forty-five miles away,
and the thing about a thrift shop is that you have to
keep stopping in regularly if you're going to find the right
sizes. I did locate a thrift shop in a town nearby, but the
children's clothes there looked just as weary as the ones
we had already. No knees to the pants. No buttons. Lots
of sweaters of that curiously *heavy* type, short but wide,
that betrays an adult size 40 in wool that sneaked through
the washer and drier on Hot. And of course no socks or
underwear or sneakers or pajamas, because those never
make it past the first wearer, and no winter coats because
you keep those for extras in your own family.

I have to hit the cut-rate chain stores.

I hate them. I hate shopping for bargains. I hate it, I

hate it, I hate it. Maybe I worked too long in department stores, in the days of my youth. I remember the ropes and the extra guards we laid on for big sales, and the ominously surging hordes of bargain hunters, their faces and elbows fierce with greed, and how sharp at nine-thirty the guards unlatched the ropes and ran like hell and the crowd came pouring in like lava, or tidal waves, savaging the counters and trampling the hesitant.

I know lots of perfectly nice people who just love a bargain. They subscribe to every newspaper in three counties to read the ads. They rise at dawn for sales. They drive endless miles. Hand-to-hand they grapple with their fellows, one on each end of a bedsheet and pulling hard, and when they win they come home flushed and tousled with successful combat. They see it as having scored a point against the gods. A victory for them, a smashing defeat for the overlords of commerce. They feel ten feet tall.

I feel like an ant. I creep around the discount stores, the kind with acres of bare aisles and no sales help and pitiless blue lighting and policemen at the exits, and I can feel my posture deteriorating. Mentally, I am wearing one of those bulging, strangely rounded tweed overcoats worn by charwomen in London, with one button hanging loose. In front of me limps a woman with a cane, an old, comfortably worn cane, and the cane has a sticker on it. The guard at the door put a sticker on it when she came in, so they would know, when she went out, that she hadn't stolen it.

Being suspected of intent to shoplift does something to me. I don't like being followed by men with revolvers, and regarded in trick mirrors, and having to check my packages. I would like to kick somebody. What makes them think I *want* their nasty merchandise? I will march back out without buying anything, which turns out to be almost impossible; you have to stand in line at the check-out counter anyway because that's the only way you can *get* out, and explain snippily to the checkout girl that you didn't find what you wanted, which she doesn't believe and her eyes go to your pocketbook, wondering what you've stuffed in there, and you try to look as if you could buy the whole store, parking lot and all, if it weren't so far below your standards, but she isn't fooled; if you had any money, you wouldn't be in a place like that to start with.

I don't *want* to be in a place like that. I yearn dreamily for stores lit by great graceful chandeliers instead of fluorescent tubes, and carpeting underfoot, and someone to ask when you can't find what you need. I want to pay two dollars for a pair of children's socks, just because they were there, and I was there, and I remembered they needed socks.

In fact, I want to buy something we don't need at all. A cocktail shaker. Flowered sheets. A piece of meat. Comfort me with pork roast for I am sick of lentils. Pursued by inflation, I am sick of lentils, spaghetti, omelets, macaroni and cheese, baked beans, tuna fish; take them away. Bring me a freezer full of old-fashioned one-piece meats. That's what I want, meat in a piece, that I can serve on a platter, and carve. (I wonder whatever happened to my carving knife?) Just to show the children. Emily remembers roast leg of lamb, but the boys are too young. In fact, the boys, otherwise reasonably bright, have never learned the *names* of different kinds of meat, and refer to them all as chicken.

Which doesn't matter; they aren't starving; but unless they get some new underwear pretty soon they'll be childless.

Underwear. Socks. Pajamas. Sneakers. I long to take them to buy sneakers in a real shoe store, where they measure your feet, and the salesman tells you to walk back and forth, and under his scrutiny you walk, solemnly, on one new sneaker and one sock, and there are tilted floor mirrors so that you as well as everyone else can see you are wearing one blue sock and one striped one.

Now we buy sneakers in places patrolled by guards but not by shoe clerks. You find what size you need by sitting down on the bare floor of the aisle and taking off one shoe, and trying on a sneaker attached to its mate by a very short tough plastic ligament. Your mother, squatting on the floor beside her pocketbook and packages, watches you walk back and forth, and the sneaker's mate, attached, thumps and bobbles at your ankle.

In the olden days you wore your new sneakers reverently home, and carried the old ones in a bag, and, if you were Emily, added them to your old-shoe collection. Now you wear the old ones and carry the new ones, still connected, home to be scissored apart. I once asked the girl at the cash register if she had anything to cut them apart with, but she didn't know what I was talking about.

When I was twenty it was fun to be broke; everyone was. I walked twenty-three blocks to work on Fridays because I didn't have bus fare, and it was sporting to have lived till payday without starving utterly to death. Now the sport has gone out of it and I'd rather be rich, and I'm awful at cutting my own hair, and my husband keeps saying, "But you wore that the *last* time we went to the Morans'."

Maybe I could get a job out here somewhere. Somewhere that I can get to the school from, when the school calls to say they have spots.

I have a vision of myself working. I am wearing a gray wool pants suit and a cream-colored shirt and talking on the phone, which I hold against my ear with my shoulder, and I'm taking notes as I talk. From time to time I glance at the clock; probably there's a meeting at two.

I consider the classified ads in the local paper. Secretaries. There are always jobs for secretaries. Memo: make Emily learn shorthand. Personally I feel too old and awkward to take up so foreign a language; I've always been rather awed by it, with its graceful loops and curls, and always disappointed when the secretary types it up, and what looked like haiku turns out to say "Enclosed please find the proof of your ad scheduled to appear on Sunday, May 12."

I am too old for a Person Friday, too.

Would it be interesting to be a Night Watchperson? How peaceful to work at night. Patrolling an empty building, swinging my nightstick or whatever (*gun?*), whistling and hearing the echo of my footsteps and whistle in the long empty corridors; trying doors to make sure they're locked. A single bright light in the parking lot, and only my own car out there, waiting for me.

On the other hand, suppose something happened? Suppose someone broke in? I am unable to summon a vision of myself subduing burglars, and holding them in a one-handed hammer lock while dialing the police with the other hand. Ben, I think, could see himself in the role, but I can't. I can barely pin a struggling five-year-old.

LADIES! Earn extra money in your spare time!

LADIES! Work at home.

Sell by phone. Tupperware parties. Sell shoes, and earn lovely fashion shoes to keep for your very own. Electrician's helper. Hairdresser. Paving contractor needs person experienced in blacktop. Plumber—first class mechanic only need apply. Mason wanted. Roofer—experienced only salary accordingly. Front End Loader Operator. Injection Press Operators. Mushroom Cutters. Well, I suppose I *could* cut mushrooms. I could learn. Siding Applicator. TOOLMAKER, MACHINIST, & CYLINDRICAL GRINDER. Maintenance—Are you Mr. Fix-it?

No.

I am abashed by how practical the employment scene is out here. Briefly, I seduce myself into believing I could Operate and Maintain Heavy Farm Machinery, but the truth is I have trouble changing tires on a light VW.

I am not employable here. No wonder I meet so many full-time housewives. The urban classified ads I was weaned on always included a lot of rather airy jobs, the kind you can talk yourself into and learn about later, but I think they'd know right away I'm not an Insulation Applicator Experienced in Batts. (Attic work, I suppose. Wear a hat so the Batts don't fly into your hair.)

I have lived in a dream world of shapeless occupations like public relations, customer contact, account executive, fashion coordinator. This is the real world: they need a mason and a plumber, and the only other jobs pay you in shoes or costume jewelry, or free extra copies of the Yellow Pages.

Driving around on my errands, I notice various houses with hand-lettered signs saying that the women there make or raise something to sell: duck eggs, quilts, fudge, Brittany spaniels, all sorts of things. I think about it, but it sounds gloomy. Sitting there day after day in my parlor surrounded by spaniels and fudge, waiting for a customer to happen down our lonely lane.

Occupation: Housewife. I am resigned.

At least in the summer we can live on tomatoes and squash. At least if it ever stops raining we can.

I get a book on raising one's own chickens, and take the matter up with my husband, explaining that they could live way, way down in the woods and he'd hardly even know they were there. He is adamant. He would know they were there, all right. He has an almost superstitious horror of things with feathers. Probably they'd escape, and find their way up to the house, and track him down from room to room, squawking and fluttering; he shudders.

Organic Gardening suggests that I raise rabbits for fun and profit and protein and, as with all its schemes, manages to make it sound plausible. A child could do it. I concentrate on the free protein and the details of building hutches, and skim through the part where you kill the babies as soon as they're weaned. At the farmers' market I buy a couple of them to try; even "dressed," which means undressed, they look quite awfully like dead rabbits. I take them home and fry and serve them; the children think they're chicken. After dinner, I explain the whole scheme.

I can still close my eyes and see the look on their faces. I don't think any of them has felt the same about me since. Not that they brood about it *constantly,* I'm sure; only that in the back of their hearts they now believe me capable of any cold-blooded horror, any imaginable atrocity; a person to stay out of lonely places with.

Slowly, the tomatoes begin to turn red. We are already sick of squash.

CHAPTER TWO

*E*mily, who has a strong sense of the natural order and fitness of things, feels we should get a puppy. Satisfied as we are with Boy, Betsey, and Sidney, people in our position, country people, require a dog. It passes through my mind, though without much conviction, that a dog might take the place of a pony, and I agree.

Matthew has gone to visit his grandmother, so Emily and Ben and I set forth to find the local SPCA, getting so severely lost the first time that we have to go home, and try again the next day, when we finally find it by accident, having taken the wrong turn.

There are cages of puppies, all dumped in cheerfully together to play, and cages of ugly orange kittens without visible futures, and cages that each contain a solitary grown dog. Emily moves back and forth in the aisle soberly inspecting puppies. One cage holds a small female sheepdog of the collie type who whines anxiously and presses against the bars for my attention. The card stapled to her cage gives her age as seven. *Seven?* Horrified, I stare down at her, and she looks up with gentle eyes and gives her tail a single questioning wag. What possible tragedy can have brought her here? She wasn't lost, and brought in by the finder, or they wouldn't be so sure of her age. Sweet-faced and mystified, she waits in her cage for the answer to be unfolded; for her people to come back to her, and have their faces kissed. If people have been your people for seven years, surely they wouldn't forget you. Surely they would come back.

I find I can't see very well, and have trouble taking an interest in Emily's puppy.

The chosen puppy is black, a girl, all curls and wiggles, and the card describes it, hopefully, as a Poodle Mix. Looks more Scottie to me. Mix, certainly. We go to fill out forms.

Several people are there in front of us, and progress is slow, impeded by phone calls, by forms lost in the files, and by a state policeman who has found a German shepherd on the highway that has to be booked in, on more forms. Ben wanders around the room poking at things. Finally I am given a form, and a pen. The form wants to know how many acres of land we own, and whether it's fenced, and if so what kind of fence, and the types and ages of our other animals, and a great deal of other curious information including, when I have printed my way down that far, the number and ages of my children.

No puppies, it says, are given for adoption into families with children under six.

Now, I am a person who obeys rules. I do what I am told. Except in obvious cases, like that ridiculous stop sign at Pine Creek Road, I obey, mostly from a strong sense of how embarrassing it would be to get caught.

On the other hand, no kid of mine tortures puppies. Not if it knows what's good for it, not at six, or five, or four. Besides, how does a puppy-torturing five-year-old change at six? You'd think it would just be hitting its stride at six. Inventing new and subtler forms, intricately psychological as well as crudely physical.

I write the twins down as six, shielding the page from the state policeman, who is still hanging around. How many years in prison for lying to the SPCA? Sealing my probable fate, I sign my name at the bottom.

The lady behind the counter reads the whole thing carefully, all the way through, including the printed questions that she must have seen before. She raises her head. She looks at Ben, patiently trying to break a lamp on the other side of the room.

"Is that your child?"

That? Of course not. Borrowed him from a friend. Found him under a cabbage. I swallow. "Yes."

"How old is he?"

Ben's a normal size for five. Matthew, who's tiny, is out of sight, at his grandmother's. Emily is standing beside me and she is looking at me to see what I am going to do. I turn my face down to the counter to keep my voice from carrying and mutter "Six," and my ears get hot.

Ben doesn't hear me. A wise-mouth kid, he'd be sure to set us straight.

The woman looks at me, and at Ben, and back at the form, and frowns. The puppy's future balances in the air.

Then she takes a pen, and scrabbles in drawers for other things to fill out and sign, and then an attendant unlocks the cage and gives us our puppy.

All the way home the puppy huddles in Emily's lap, trembling, and Ben leans over the seat to touch her from time to time. I glance down sourly; she seems to me to have been morally expensive.

At home, released, she goes mad with joy over grass and leaves and bits of stick after the concrete cage, and the children roll on the lawn with her. It's all very cute. Watching, I wish she was the little collie. I wish we had brought the little collie home instead, and tried to bring some light into her mysteriously darkened life.

As time goes on, there seem to be more and more of those things that I should have done, and didn't, and they don't get any easier to recognize at the time, either.

PETS COMPLICATE LIFE. THEY TEND TO SNOWBALL, TOO; if you have some already, you tend to get more, and each additional one complicates life a little further. I know some people who don't have any at all and never did, and if you don't have *any*, then you don't get *more*. It's like smoking. Your kid wins a goldfish at a birthday party, and you figure, since you've already got a goldfish, you might as well have an Irish wolfhound and a coatimundi and a pair of indigo snakes and before you know it you can charge admission and sell tickets. The trick is not to start in the first place, but by the time you realize that it's too late.

Fish tanks and gerbil cages have to be cleaned. Birds

throw bird seed on the floor, and also, at least in our house, tend to die inexplicably and be found in the morning with their stiff little claws in the air, and have to be buried in shoe boxes. Dogs throw up on the rug and leave dog hairs on the couch. Cats throw up on the rug, leave cat hairs on the couch, and shred the arms of the chairs until gray stuffing leaks out disgustingly.

Lots of people who really hate animals keep them anyway because they're good for the children. They teach children responsibility and the facts of life, or so it is said. Responsibility is taught by having your parents say, "It's your dog and if you can't clean up after it we'll have to get rid of it." This seems a bit tough on the dog, since junior's future citizenship isn't *its* problem, and what junior is learning, if anything, is probably a lot of dark and complicated things about parents, and the treacherous nature of birthday presents.

Learning the facts of life calls for a female cat or dog with access to gents; thus mom and dad won't have to explain where babies come from, since the kids can learn where puppies come from and draw the appropriate inferences. Then junior has to find homes for the puppies. This turns out to be the most memorable, because longest and hardest, part of the process, and twenty years from now there's junior, thoroughly confused, knocking on doors with a basket full of babies.

It's embarrassing, but I happen to like having animals around. I pretend they're there to teach my children things, because animals are considered a perverse taste in a full-grown housewife with three kids. Animals are for the childless; it is right and proper for them to get attached, even desperately attached, to the creatures they keep, but for us mothers the children themselves are supposed to take the place of pets.

"I keep telling the kids," says my neighbor, "if their kitten doesn't stay out of my sewing things, I'm taking it to be put to sleep. And I am, too."

And she is, too. I nod sycophantically, wondering how it would feel to prefer a spool of thread to a kitten playing. Is she nuts? Am I? Worse: what manner of worm am I to pretend I agree with her? And how can she pretend to believe I agree with her, as she sits on that shredded chair with dog hairs all over her backside?

Sidney got hit by a car.

Only about three cars a day go down our lane, and slowly, because of the potholes, so a cat tends to forget about cars. Besides, this is the country, and people who would drive into a tree rather than hit someone's hunting dog can run over any number of cats without pausing. Cats don't count. You keep some in the barn, for the rats, but there are always plenty.

I rushed him, moaning dreadfully through his splintered jaw, to the vet. It was going to be an expensive business, obviously, and this was a country vet; he knew what a watchdog was worth, or a handy-hunter-over-fences, or a prize Guernsey. I didn't want him to think this ordinary alley cat with the crooked black mustache was in any way, well, *expendable*.

"Please do everything you can," I croaked. "He's the children's pet. The children are very fond of him." I wiped some tears off the bunny-soft fur. Suppose he never came into the kitchen again, this foolish, innocent-hearted cat, to ask about dinner with his fat soft tail making question marks in the air? What would the house be like without Sidney? He isn't Boy, of course; a world without Boy does not bear thinking of; but he is Sidney, sweet Sidney, and our only cat that plays the piano. Imagine never waking up at 4 A.M. to hear Sidney rippling off arpeggios in the dark downstairs. Imagine nights without Sidney at 5 A.M. reluctantly, almost apologetically, throwing my alarm clock and bedside lamp on the floor so I will rise and let him out.

"The children would be very upset," I muttered hoarsely, and groped my way blindly to the door.

I don't think responsibility is a taught subject, like multiplication, gradually memorized by kids each time they change the kitty-litter pan, and my children can jolly well learn the facts of life on the school bus like everyone else. We have animals because they live here. They are part of the circle, the more-or-less round and often faulty, staticky electrical current known as the family.

Taking care of animals and cleaning up after them, now an optional piece of housewifery, used to be a proper and inevitable part, and creative (eggs, milk, transportation, bacon) rather than janitorial (puddles, shedding, the crunch of Cat Chows on the kitchen floor). I think I would have liked that. I'd rather feed the pigs than a lot of things I do around here. I am tempted to go on accumulating animals, more and more and more, until I'm so busy I couldn't possibly stop to scrub the children's bathtub. I could get Matthew his cow. They could sit in the driveway together gazing mildly around at the summer air; I could learn to milk.

Luckily my husband has better sense. He stopped me from bringing home a goat named Sheba the other day, a goat with long satin ears and that jaded, cosmopolitan expression goats have, rightly assuming it would end up in the living room.

In addition to the regularly scheduled pets, children bring in extras. In the city they bring in starving kittens for which homes must be found, and pigeons dying of some disease probably fatal to humans. In the country they bring in frogs, toads, snakes, box turtles with furious little red eyes, lizards, shrews, lightning bugs, and bewildered baby robins. Inexpertly housed in grocery-store cartons, they either perish and have to be buried, or escape and pose special housekeeping problems of their own. No one told you in school that you would spend a significant part of your adult life lying with your cheek pressed to the dusty floor, squinting under a bed and poking hopefully with the mop handle for a missing newt, one of the slippery little red ones that live under rocks. Or blundering around in your nightie after the lightning bugs escaped from a jelly jar, while Benjamin wrings his hands and weeps.

Sometimes your pets bring in pets. Betsey brought home, carefully, a very small garter snake and gave it to me, and we named it Louise and kept it in a fishbowl. Sometimes Emily wore it as a bracelet.

Boy brought home a baby rabbit.

My husband had gone to drive some guests to the train station, a ceremony proper to country life, and left me to entertain an urbane and charming musician friend from New York. Boy brought the rabbit in and released it, graciously, at our feet.

The other two cats and the dog sprang to attention. The rabbit gave a small shriek of understandable concern and scooted under the couch. The musician friend gave a much louder shriek, and scrambled up and stood on the couch. The dog and all three cats leaped for the rabbit and knocked their heads together. The rabbit shot out and ran brainlessly in circles. A lamp fell over.

"Quick," I yelled, "you grab the rabbit while I hold the dog!"

"Are you *kidding?*" cried the friend. He clutched his figurative skirts around him and took a deep breath to scream again.

I howled up the stairs for Emily. She appeared in pajamas and, waked from a sound sleep, grasped the problem at once. Between us we separated the livestock, while the friend continued to stand on the couch and scream unhelpfully. Things like this never happened in his apartment on West Forty-fifth Street.

I carried the rabbit, still in mint condition except its poor nerves, out to the woods and sent it home, and came back and picked up the furniture and a lot of cigarette butts and things, and gave my guest some brandy. Probably the rabbit should have had some too.

Boy, unoffended, washed his paws. I don't think he'd expected to be allowed to keep it; it was just to show.

IN THE BEGINNING, WE HAD THOUGHT ABOUT INVITING out our friends from town. How nice for them, we said smugly, to have a country place to go and visit, weekends in the summer. Presently we came to realize that all our friends who had the smallest interest in the country had already moved to it, and the ones still in towns were there because they liked it there, and were mortally afraid of snakes in the tall grass. Rabbits under the couch.

"NOW, CHILDREN," I SAID, AND GOT OUT A PENCIL AND paper, "what shall we name the puppy?"

"Vicky," said my husband, and turned a page.

"*Vicky?* Why Vicky?"

"I don't like that," objected Emily.

"Her name could be Lassie," said Matthew.

"Spot," I offered.

"Wiggles," said Ben.

"Mabel," I said. "She looks like a Mabel. Winifred. Mildred."

My husband glanced up briefly. "Her name's Vicky."

We settled down to the business of toilet-training Vicky. I spent a lot of time, that rainy summer, standing on the lawn holding an umbrella over her, rain trickling off it down my collar, and speaking in falsetto tones of encouragement. She would turn her anxious whiskery face up to me with reproach. Whatever mad combination of genes has created this mixture of dogs, she is no Boy Scout. She is a parlor dog, a sofa dog. She curls up one damp front paw and looks at me in deepest gloom from under her drooping eyebrows, and shivers. The arrangements seem to her, clearly, uncivilized. Primitive.

"She wants a doggy-litter pan," said Emily.

The people in this area know a lot about breeds of dogs, and when Vicky appears in public they always ask me, politely, what kind of dog she is. Eventually I get tired of apologizing and take to saying she is a Hedge Terrier, still rare in this country, originally bred in England to chase the sparrows out of hedgerows; it's hard to imagine her chasing anything bigger.

From the beginning she was an elderly, neurotic puppy, afraid of thunderstorms and burglars and strange cats. Emily's idea to begin with, she attached herself to me like a tick. If I turned around suddenly, I fell over her. If I stopped suddenly, she bumped into my ankles. She waited for me outside the bathroom door; I could hear her breathing. She slept with me.

Boy was disgusted. Too proud to compete for attention, he could only sit with his back to me, hoping I would notice his grief.

CHAPTER THREE

The summer moves on, pouring rain, and the beginning of school edges into sight.

Because of my working, the twins have spent their lives, beginning half an hour after they were housebroken, in the all-day private nursery schools patronized by working mothers. Juice time, nap time, with one's name-tagged blankets spread out on the floor, easel painting, song time, and Simon Says do not quite take up the full day, so a certain amount of education creeps in to kill time.

The previous fall Benjamin, because of a tendency to hit very small people, was moved up, age four, to the kindergarten class, many of whose members were turning six and losing their front teeth. After a brief unequal battle with the staff, Matthew packed up his crayons and followed Ben. All hands are now reading noisily from cereal boxes, traffic signs, and other pre-primers, and have developed a boring interest in mathematics. "S-T-O-P spells stop, yes, Mommy? Five and five make ten, right, Mommy? *Right, Mommy?* RIGHT, MOMMY?"

This fall they are eligible for the afternoon kindergarten at the local public school, where they will learn all over again to tell a circle from a triangle as a preparation for telling A from B. When Ben is bored he socks people. When Matt is bored he practices standing on his head and making faces.

When Mommy has both of them in school but a scant three hours a day, she stands on her head and makes faces *and* socks people.

It also develops that, while the school bus will bring them home along with everyone else when school is over, I am responsible for getting them there at twelve-fifteen, a marvelously inconvenient hour to make a fourteen-mile round trip.

I call the school and get some local names, and try to find someone to share the driving with. No luck. All the car pools are full, sorry. The other mothers all know each other and made their arrangements long ago, and what sort of slob am I to have left it so late?

I feel inadequate, and long to go to a sales promotion meeting. I want to sit at a polished table with a sharpened pencil and a pad of lined yellow paper, and make intelligent suggestions. I want to tell someone, "Hold my calls." I want to throw paper at the wastebasket and miss; I want to do something I know *how* to do.

Instead, I drive my children to the public school and try to remember when, if ever, they had their tetanus shots. Measles, rubella, polio vaccine, and what kind of polio vaccine, and how many times. I don't know. I always thought shots were something the pediatrician took care of. I didn't realize they were my responsibility. I feel about five years old. Rattled, I make up a lot of dates, and it turns out the rubella vaccine wasn't even *invented* then.

The school sits on a hill just beyond the village, commanding a heart-stopping view of rolling fields and hills and Chester County bank barns, but you can't fool me. The inside gives it away. It all comes back to me. The smell of the halls. The particular sound one's feet make in the halls of a school. The ferocity of the librarian. The cynicism of the nurse. The expression of trapped loathing on the face of the kindergarten teacher, who looks well past retirement age and desperate. She fixes me with a stony little eye and says, "Do you realize there are *fifteen* boys in this class, and only seven girls?"

She clearly feels this is my fault. So do I.

She looks down, down, at tiny Matthew, and says, "Tuck your shirt in, young man. In this class, we keep our shirts tucked in."

The principal seems relaxed and pleasant, but this is only a mask, *I* know what principals are like. *I* know what he's going to do to my children, the minute I leave.

I smirk placatingly and offer them Emily, in compensation for the twins. All three are sucked into the state's official school system and disappear, and this much of their lives is now out of my hands. I think nostalgically of our private schools in town, where we were paying customers and set our feet down firmly in the halls, and everyone knew that if we didn't like it we would leave.

Shamelessly I flee the building. There is my beautiful, beautiful old car waiting for me, and lo, I am grown up and can drive away, and I hurry toward it with light steps and make my escape, leaving hostages behind.

In spite of what i have read to the contrary, public school seems not to have changed at all since the forties. There are synonyms and antonyms, and a Book Fair, and Hygiene, and intramurals and what-I-had-for-breakfast, a question that always, in any generation, gets asked on the one day you were out of eggs and bread and they had cold baked beans and ginger ale. Papers come home to fill out and return, and sign here if you want the twins to study a band instrument. Just what we've always needed.

Ben says, "We learned a new song in school today. It goes, 'A penny for a pocket weasel.' Do you know that song?"

I say that I do, and for a dizzy moment I can't think of any other words to it. The pocket weasel joins my ghostly caravan, but being so little it's really no trouble at all.

Ben gets chicken pox, and loses a tooth, and the Tooth Fairy, in an anti-inflationary gesture, leaves a dime under his pillow. Matt gets chicken pox and is much sicker and so astonishingly spotty for so long that I have trouble with the school nurse. We have a fight over the phone, which I win by saying that if she wants him to go back home she'll have to bring him herself.

Afternoons are the wrong time to go to school. It leaves the mornings blank.

One morning, Matthew said that he was the plumber and my sink was broken, and crawled under it with some cute little toy plastic tools. Presently he let out a yell and said water was pouring out. *I* let out a yell, and hauled him out from under and squeezed in myself, crouching in water and Clorox bottles, frantically turning knobs.

Ben let out a yell and said, "The house is flooding, the house is flooding, I gotta get out of here!" and flung himself into the front storm door, shattering it into thousands of long wicked scimitars of glass. Strangely, none of them cut his throat from ear to ear.

After I mop up the water and sweep up the glass and change into dry jeans, it is time to make sandwiches and drive them to school.

Actually this trip, while a nuisance, is so damned adorable it soothes me; I keep driving into ditches gawking out the window. I am still basically city folk. A tilted field with sheep in it, with a creek winding along the bottom and an old stone barn, still charms the socks off me. The boys tell me the school bus uses this same road, which is eight feet wide and paved only in spots. I find it hard to believe. If I ever *met* the school bus on it, I would abandon the car and climb a tree.

I leave the boys at school, and come home wondering, every day, if the bus will really bring them back, or if maybe the arrangements have been secretly changed and no one told me.

I can still hear Emily crying in the vestibule. Transportation is a nightmare; it preys on my mind.

I walk around the house with the uneasy conviction that somewhere, on some rainy roadside or in front of some locked building, a child is waiting for me in deepening despair, right this very minute. I keep counting children in my head. Ben is upstairs in bed with a cold; in ten minutes it is time to drive Matthew to school (comb hair, check shoelaces, *tuck in shirt*) (Could I pin it to his pants inside? Paste it to his flesh?) and Ben will have to come too (dress warmly) so as not to be left alone. Emily will not be home on the bus because it's Tumbling this afternoon (pick up at four). Matthew will be home on the bus at three-forty, then put instantly into the car (with Ben; dress warmly) and driven straight back to school to pick up Emily (after Tumbling) and I can pick up milk and eggs and scotch on the way back. I have not left any children anywhere by accident. No one is standing on a deserted sidewalk with an instrument case after a music lesson, or in front of a barn with a hard hat after a riding lesson, waiting. No one. Then I go upstairs to make sure the two at home really are at home. They are, and have made a booby trap out of clothesline and all the clean bath towels, and are hiding under the bed waiting for me to fall in it.

Slowly, like thumbscrews, life gets more complicated with each passing month. I am terrified of forgetting things. Losing one of the pieces. Nothing in a housewife's life connects together in any logical order, so you just have to keep counting the different pieces over and over. Making lists.

THE TROUBLE WITH HOUSEWIFERY ISN'T REALLY TOO *much* to do, it's too many different *kinds* of things. One thing does not lead to another. Which is why you keep forgetting to get a birthday present for Davey's party Saturday. You remembered butter and grass seed, took the dog to the vet, checked the oil in the car, and called the plumber, but none of these things reminded you of birthday presents.

You have to make a list. A list is an emotional crutch, giving you a phony sense of control over the unmanageable bits of your life. Lists are written on envelopes or matchbooks, in crayon, Magic Marker, or lipstick. Lipstick is the worst. It sinks into matchbooks and spreads, like initials in a beech tree, till you can't tell whether to buy milk or call Mike or maybe do something with mice.

The list is supposed to tell you what you have to do, but it can only tell you some of it. It doesn't tell you to take the wash out and put it in the drier. You have to remember that all by yourself, usually at a quarter of eight the next morning, when nobody has any socks and there they still are, twisted into a multicolored rope fermenting at the bottom of the washer. Then you have to dry them in the oven, with people mumbling into their cereal about how even Susan *Crandall*'s mother gets her *socks* dry.

You can't write down, "Put wash in drier." People can't live like that, and it would take reams of paper, and leave no time for the jobs themselves. You have to hit the high points, and hope the other things will somehow attach themselves to the ones you did write down. You develop a kind of shorthand that men, whose lives are simpler, find entertaining.

"What's this?" he says. "It's in blue crayon, on one of Ben's arithmetic papers."

"That's mine," you say. "Give it to me, I was looking all over for it."

"Wait a minute, wait a minute. What's it mean? Look, it says 'Wents Thur.' What on earth is Wents Thur? Sounds like a town in England. Some place with a ruined Norman church. 'W. drinks. Scotch? Check.' "

You sigh. "The Wentworths are coming for dinner Thursday, and I can't decide what to have. And I need something to serve first, with drinks. 'W. drinks' doesn't mean Wentworth drinks, in spite of the way he carried on that time with the piano; it means '*with* drinks.' Only he certainly can put it away, so I meant to see how much scotch we have, and if we need more I'll have to cash a check. Okay?"

"I see Ben missed four out of ten arithmetic problems," he says, glancing at the other side. "I'm going to have a talk with that young man. What does 'Sitter sat' mean, then? What has the sitter done if she hasn't sat? Why write *that* down?"

"Oh, give me that, will you? 'Sitter sat' means I have to call Joan for Saturday night because we're going to that meeting, and if you want to wear your gray suit I'll have to get it to the cleaners by tomorrow, and stop on the way to get some TV dinners for the kids. That's what it means."

"I don't see why you can't write standard English," he says loftily, handing it over. "No wonder Ben's having trouble. It's probably hereditary."

Naturally, if you wrote it all out in standard English, it would look more like a book than a list and take so long to read the cleaner would be closed before you got there. You abbreviate. If you catch it fast enough, sometimes you even remember what the abbreviations meant. It resembles shorthand in that you cannot let it get cold; a list must be used while its hidden meanings are still warm and fresh.

Nothing is more disconcerting than to find, while digging for your car keys, a scrap of paper that says something like "SCHOOL!!"

Well, did you do it? You lean your forehead on the steering wheel and try to remember. It was important. Look at the exclamation points. Some child's whole future hung quivering there. An urgent consultation with the teacher? Or, heavens, with the *principal*? And you never showed up, and the child has been expelled? Or was it to pick someone up at school after hockey practice or band, and you never did and they're still standing there, clutching gym shoes or flute, waiting, weeks later? No, they were all around at breakfast this morning. Something to sign and return? Lost by now, certainly. A PTA meeting? No, that wouldn't have exclamation points. Some medical certificate to get filled out? A committee you joined? A committee you were *chairman* of, and forgot all about? Notebook paper to buy? The class play, and you never made a costume? Or even went?

You'll never know. At the moment you wrote it, the mere act of writing it down gave you a feeling of having dealt responsibly with the matter, and you promptly forgot it. This is one of the problems of the list-maker.

Another problem is remembering to consult them. This

is actually the hardest part. Anyone can write a list, but it takes a really collected housewife to look at it later. You have too many things to do to sit around looking at lists and finding out what you have to do. This is bad. The first thing on your list was "Books to libry," and the library closed at noon. (They charge for Sundays, too.) A well-consulted list helps one arrange priorities, so that the most urgent things get done first and the less urgent don't get done at all, but can be transferred to the next list you write, after the first is tattered to illegibility.

This is called a running list. If you're stubborn, you can keep undone things moving from list to list more or less forever. If you are more resigned to the workings of fate and the fallibility of the human race, you can stop re-copying them after six months or so. If you haven't called Marge by now, she'd probably hang up on you anyway. Besides, you were going to call to ask after her pregnancy, and the kid must be in kindergarten by now.

Grocery lists, of course, are the commonest kind, and come in two styles. There are grocery lists tucked in among other things to do, involving emergency items, things you've run out of and things you need for what you're making for the Wentworths: coat from clnrs, p.u. pix, sour cream, bread, call Marge, shortening, lv car shop adj. timing, scotch. Then there are the grocery lists for your major shopping of the week.

I've seen really efficient ladies shopping with their lists. They carry the list, *and* a pencil, with a point on it, or a pen that still actually makes marks, and after each purchase they cross the item off. (They carry little pocket calculators, too. This is a swell idea, but can you imagine what the twins could do to one? No, I couldn't hide it; they can *smell* things like that.) These ladies also own a list pad with a hard backing on it, so they don't have to use their knees, or ask a passing shopper to bend over so they can write on her back.

These ladies must always shop at the same store, so they can put the list in order. As everyone knows, a random list is exhausting although a good way to lose twenty pounds. "Eggs," it says, and eggs are in the refrigerator in the farthest corner from the door; "beans," and beans are in aisle 4; "vermouth," and the liquor store is three blocks down and turn left on Bridge Street. I think what these efficient ladies do is, first, they write down everything they need, and then they take a fresh piece of paper and arrange it all in the order of its appearance in the supermarket, starting to the right of the aisle by the door. Goodness knows when they find time to shower and dress.

They list the vermouth separately, of course. They list the other errands in order of *their* appearance, too.

I used to do that in the city. I did things on the way home from work, in order: "E's shoes from rpr shp, p.u. M's prescription, sugar soap tuna fish, mail chk." In the country, everything I do is ten miles away in the opposite direction. Also a lot of new things have appeared on the list: "E riding lesson Goshen 2:30, p.u. 3:30, p.u. M ballfield P'ville 4, see man chain saw Rte 29 left at orchard sign, spray for apple trs Sp. City, lwn mwr to shop Creek Road." Arrangement here makes no difference.

You wouldn't believe there were so many points to the compass.

Some people, writing a grocery list, put down everything they need, even bread. Some people just list the things they don't buy every week, like baking powder and eggplant. My husband adheres to the first creed, or at least he thinks I should. He thinks a grocery list should be so comprehensive that a total stranger could walk in and pick it up off the kitchen table and go shopping for you. (Total strangers rarely do. If they did, I'd be glad to list everything, including my previous addresses.)

He also thinks I should be able to sit down over my second cup of coffee and list from memory everything we're out of or will be. This is ridiculous. There'd be no room left in my head for the really important things, like who's ahead in the National League and where Ben put his homework. When I see the damn thing in the grocery store, I will know I need it. I hope. It requires a kind of tranced state, and total concentration, and the children left at home locked in a closet or something instead of dragging at my clothing and whining for candy-flavored cereal. I try to shop alone, and walk slowly and think hard, and not answer when spoken to.

Once every blue moon my husband actually does the shopping for me, using my list, and then he says, "But you didn't *say* to buy cat food. How was I supposed to know? Why didn't you write it down?" And I point out reasonably that he forgot to buy three items that I *did* write down, so what would have been the use? And then

he says—well, I don't think it's any of your business what
we say then.

Another problem with the grocery list is that you can't
always tell ahead of time. I mean, they're having a beef
sale, and you decide to get a brisket and have a nice pot
roast, which means you'd better get garlic, and carrots.
But when you get there they have only two briskets left,
and they look dismal, so you decide on hamburger instead, and that means hamburger buns and relish instead
of garlic and carrots.

I've tried giving up grocery lists entirely and relying on
intuition, but this leads to other forms of trouble. Once
you've run out of napkins and light bulbs, for instance,
and spent a week with everyone grumbling about paper
towels at dinner, and crouching around a single light to
read like Abe Lincoln at the fireside, you find you can't
stop buying them. Every time you see a display of napkins,
messages flicker in your brain like heat lightning, and you
gather them by the armful.

After a while you have to keep the canned goods on
the floor because all the shelves are full of light bulbs and
napkins.

Then the day comes when it gets through to you,
and you go to the store and say, "Well, at least I know
we don't need napkins or light bulbs," and this compla-
cent sense of abundance persists until long after you've
run out again, and everyone's clustering around the
candles.

Non-food items are the hardest to keep in mind without a list. Food has a certain rhythm. For once, one thing

leads to another. Hamburger leads to buns. But things you aren't going to actually put on a plate and serve, like soap, should be listed, as well as auxiliary food like pepper and salad oil.

There's a lot to be said for crossing things off as you buy them. It helps identify an inoperative list. Few things are more frustrating than coming home from the store, full of satisfaction at a job well done, to find you have purchased last week's groceries.

To cross things off, you need, as noted previously, a list pad with a hard back and something that writes. Unless these are in some way fastened tightly to your pocketbook, however, your daughter will draw horses on every page and your sons will use the pencil to punch another hole in their belts. But if they *are* chained to your pocketbook, it's inconvenient to jot things down as they occur to you. You have to go trailing your pocketbook around the house, dripping pennies.

My husband once bought me a plastic memo board as big as a bath towel to hang up in the kitchen and write things on, like "Call Ann! mop sponge, TV man." It was too big to go in my pocketbook and too dangerous to carry if it was windy out, in case of being swept off into the next county, so it couldn't really go shopping with me; I would have to copy everything down from it onto an old envelope before I went to the store. I did try, but after a while the twins scribbled on it with something indelible and I threw it away. (How come everything *they* write with is permanent, and can't be removed by bleach or razor blade or the winds of time, while nothing *I* write with will identify a person's lunch box for more than two days?)

Lists multiply at a fairly constant rate most of the time, but they do have special breeding seasons when they simply burst into fertility, like fleas. There's the beginning of school: "Gym suit E, gmmd reinforcements, bk covers, snkers M, coats from clnr, conf. M's teacher, make app dr. checkup all, eye dr. B, 3-ring paper, apron home ec E, dimes frm bnk mlk mny, note to tchr B, thermos, haircuts Sat."

And Christmas. Oh, boy, Christmas. My lists. *Their* lists, and their revised lists. When I was a child, we wrote lists of requests to Santa Claus and burned them ceremoniously in the fireplace. As a system of mail delivery it seems not inferior to the public one, and it kept the house from getting cluttered up, but my own pragmatic young simply hand their lists to me, and I put them in my pocketbook where they mingle freely with my own. Separate grocery lists for cookie ingredients, and for parties. Lists of my friends, lists of *their* friends, card lists, invitation lists, things to be mailed, wrapping paper, chk tree lights, Xmas play Fri 19th 7 pm, M at schl by 6:40, CROWN, construc. paper, invites party, cards, concert E 22nd, stamps P.O., Aunt L here 22–24 p.u. station 11:20, cln gst rm, kinder prgrm Wed 10 AM, holly? stockings.

And all the time, underneath them in the pocketbook lies the substrata of the usual lists, because life goes on: "dog shots vet Wed., call Marge, cornstarch lemons sandwich bags, return snow shovel, Wents dinner Tues."

Some Christmas lists even have to be hidden, but if

you've put them where the kids can't find them it's a cinch you can't either. The best place to hide them is in your pocketbook, among the other lists. Looks like a wastebasket in there.

At Christmas, the law of diminishing returns sets in. It takes longer to find the right list than it would to sit still and wait for the things on it to drift into your mind. It seems to me that in the hours I'd save not making lists, or looking for them, I could do all my shopping and make cookies and have time left over to master calculus, or take a course in ceramics.

I can't quit, though. List-making is addictive. A psychological dependency builds up. When you realize you're running out of salt, or haven't mailed the presents for your sister's children, a terrible panic grips you if it isn't written down. Quick, a pencil. Well, okay, a crayon. It's a yellow crayon and doesn't show, but you use it anyway. Paper. There isn't any, so you use the margin on the newspaper, and write on it with yellow crayon: "salt mail pres N's kids." Even immediately after writing it you can't possibly read it, but a great flood of relief washes over you. Relaxed, secure, and happy, you tear out the smudgy little gray scrap and drop it into your pocketbook. Along with all the other scraps.

Now nothing can be overlooked, no tragedy shall befall you, your home will run like clockwork and the days roll smoothly forward. You are organized. Efficient. You are on top of it all, in perfect control of all the whirling little splintery pieces of your world; you have made a list.

CHAPTER FOUR

*I*n addition to all the things you have to do, there are all the things you gradually come to *own*. As a slip of a girl, wandering on my own from apartment to apartment, I could pack my entire life into three cartons from the liquor store, and often did. Housewives accumulate. Their husbands bring home patented bottle openers and forty-year-old novels by ladies with three names that they found for a dime in a stall. Their children bring home interesting stones from the roadside and drawings from school and plastic models of horses and other people's sweaters.

Clothes are the worst. They pile up until the closets buckle. Horrible clothes. Shrunken, faded, unraveling, buttonless, mysteriously stained, but recognizably clothes. T-shirts on which someone has lettered, crookedly, SUPPERMAN. Mateless socks by the score. Sneakers whose uppers have separated almost but not quite entirely from the soles. I ought to throw the stuff away, regularly, systematically, as it becomes unwearable, but it hurts me to pitch it into the trash. It feels sinful, like throwing a book in the fire. Instead, I look vaguely around for someone to *give* it to, and nobody wants it, so I put it away until somebody does, and now there's really too *much* to throw away. Too much work, too many bags full.

In the city, throwing things out was easier. No matter how large or disagreeable it was, if you put it out on the sidewalk someone stole it, often before you were back in the house. (Sometimes it was Emily who stole it, and there it was home again.) But in the country you have to pay a man with a truck to come take *anything* away. Or you can throw it out the window into the back yard; a lot of people do. Or into someone else's yard. Anyway, I don't; I keep it. All of it.

Other people have old trunks in which to store their summer things for the winter, and vice versa, and besides they have cellars and attics to store them *in* in their trunks. Our attic is a triangular area through a trapdoor and it's lined with that asbestos fluff that gives you black lung or whatever, and the house is built on a concrete slab, and I don't have any old trunks. So I put everything into a lot of grocery bags and stick the tops together with tape, and it looks pretty tacky in the closets. The bags are always bursting open and disgorging a lot of sunsuits in January, all over my shoes. In spring and fall I take things out by degrees, and put other things in by degrees, and everything gets thoroughly jumbled and tangled. When it gets to about October, everything's pretty much out in the open except the actual bathing suits and the actual snowpants, and bureau drawers are overflowing with the stuff, none of which ever seems quite right for that day's weather. October is like that. Usually.

"Wake up," said my husband, at five forty-five.

"Why?" I took his abandoned pillow and fitted it tightly over my head to signify unwillingness.

"Because it's a winter wonderland out there, that's what it is. Must be six inches of snow."

"Don't be silly, that's moonlight," I snapped muffledly. "It's October. I think. Yes, it's October."

"It looks like snow to me," he said, and went downstairs, and I floated back off to sleep. Presently he came upstairs again and said, "I had a lot of trouble with Vicky. She won't go out in the snow. She just stands there and cries."

I couldn't think of the right answer to that so I pretended to be asleep. Which I was, really. After a while I heard his car struggling in the driveway and then going away in the dark.

At seven-thirty Emily's alarm went off, and she woke me because my alarm clock had been broken for a month and I kept forgetting to buy it those fancy little batteries. "What are you doing with a pillow on your head?" she asked reasonably. "How can you breathe? Get up, it's snowing, hard, and there's snow all over everything."

"I'm *getting* up," I said, from underneath.

Five minutes later she called from her room, "Are you up yet? I don't know what time it is because my clock just stopped."

That woke me. I reached quickly for the bedside lamp

and pressed its switch: nothing. Muttering, I found my slippers and bathrobe and headed for the bathroom. I heard a child in the other bathroom, and shouted, "Don't flush the toilet!" just barely too late.

The tap wheezed and sighed at my toothbrush but no water came out. No power: no pump.

"Shit," I whispered sincerely, and went downstairs with my mouth full of fur.

Downstairs was dim and gray. I found some matches and lit the candles on the dinner table and a candle shaped like a horse's head that Emily got for her birthday. No power: no light. I considered the effect for a while and then went upstairs and got dressed.

In their room the boys were complaining that their lights wouldn't go on so how could they get dressed? I told them to go back to bed, then, and went downstairs and outside into the winter wonderland. My boots were packed away in a bag somewhere, and the snow was over the tops of my loafers and well up my ankles. My husband's tracks and skid marks were already blurred. The woodpile was under six inches of wet snow, and lots more was falling in a brisk, determined way. Luckily, being a homesteader, I had put some logs and kindling in the garage against just such a moment, so I got a fire started, and dragged in some wet snowy logs to dry in front of it, the whole process letting a lot of cold air into the rapidly chilling house. No power: no heat.

My husband had made some coffee and left it on the stove; it was, of course, cold. No power: no stove. I set the pot in the fireplace to warm up.

"Will there be school?" asked Emily. "Will they close the school?"

"I don't know." Outside it was quiet and dim, and the snow fell, and no cars went down the lane; nothing moved but the snow. "Go get Daddy's transistor radio, it's in the bathroom."

The radio wasn't very helpful. In the warm city it had rained all night, and was still raining. I couldn't find any local stations; they're like four-leaf clovers; you really have to know where to look. The news from the city was so irrelevant that it made me feel abandoned, and desolate, and cross, so I turned it off.

"I suppose there's school," I said. "Maybe they've plowed the highway. Your face is dirty."

"There isn't any water."

"Wash it with snow."

She went outside and washed her face in snow, and ate some cold cereal, and went off to wait for the school bus, looking forlorn under the great trees in the falling snow.

I took the largest pot, the one I boil corn in, and filled it with snow. From the woods came the splintering crack and crash of branches. The vegetable garden, the part that stuck up through the snow, was gray and shriveled. So much for the promising young endive, the fall lettuce, the last of the tomatoes. So much for the spinach. In the woods, most of the leaves hadn't even turned yet, and the green forest covered with snow had a sinister look, as if the enemy had sent a secret weapon. The red maple by the porch was broken in half.

I set the pot full of snow on the hearth. The boys came downstairs griping.

"What'd you light the candles for? It's not dinner time."

"Yeah. What'd you light the candles for? You got candles all over."

Even with candles, the room was gray. I have sometimes thought that life before electric lights might have been pleasant; a softer, quieter sort of life, kind to the wrinkles and sharp edges of things, conducive to reflection. It wasn't really. It was depressing, with a sense of twilight leaking into everything, like autumn in the Arctic Circle. There were some kerosene lamps on the table on the porch, and I went out to fetch them, and on my way through the parlor I remembered what my husband said about Vicky not wanting to go out. She had left not one but two large puddles on the floor and a good-sized pile of shit on the rug.

I scolded her, and dragged her to the door and opened it. "Outside," I said. "Bad dog. *Outside!*"

She looked up at me, and out at the snow, and back at me. Her ears fell. She crouched, and started to shake all over. She thought it was her fault. Her mess out there. Her epic, all-encompassing mess she had somehow made, and for which she deserved nothing less than death. Trembling, she clung to the floor and waited for the blows.

"Hey," said Ben. "Where's breakfast?"

"Can I watch television till breakfast?" asked Matt.

"You can have Apple Jacks for breakfast," I said generously. Apple Jacks and suchlike children's products I have ruled to be not breakfast, not food, acceptable only as a rather low-grade snack; deprived, they mumble gloomily into their eggs and toast. No power: no eggs and toast. But even Apple Jacks for breakfast don't make up for "Sesame Street." No power: no telly.

By this time the fire had taken hold and the coffee, as I burned my hand dragging it out, was boiling merrily. I drank some. It was evil. The snow in the pot had shrunk into a withered ball, with a little sooty water around it, and I brushed my teeth with it, dodging ashes.

The phone rang. I stared at it, astonished that this one lifeline was still attached to our drifting raft; we will freeze and starve here in the dark, but the phone, of all things, still works.

It was our neighbor Horace, a local pioneer type, wanting to know if we had wood and water. I bristled. I may look like city folk to you, mister, but at heart I am a homesteader. Yes, we have wood, and I am melting snow for water; do I get my scout badge?

He said not to melt snow, he had plenty of water for us.

"What do you do, pump it by hand?"

Yes; he had an emergency hand pump, and would bring me all the water I wanted.

I said I liked melting snow. How can I earn my homesteader points if the grownups are going to keep dropping by to help?

Horace went on to explain which tree had fallen over the power line, and where, and how the blackout had spread throughout the whole valley area. Restless, my sons came in to watch me on the phone, as usual, and ask questions.

I held my hand over the phone and hissed, "Look out where you're *stepping*."

"What?" said Matt, stepping back into Vicky's pile on the rug.

"Just stand *still*," I groaned. I didn't really want Horace to know we were shin-deep in dog turds; it was bad for my image.

"Why does he have to stand still?" asked Ben, walking through one of the puddles.

"*Don't move, either of you.*" I put as much venom into my voice as is possible when out of striking distance, fastened to a phone. Horace went on to explain how no one else from here to Phoenixville had thought to call the power company, and how it took him twenty minutes to get through to them.

Ben went over to check the snow from the window, leaving generous footprints. "Boy, look at it snow," he said, and Matt hurried to a different window, by a different route, leaving his own footprints. "Can we make a snowman?" he asked. "Mom? Mom, I *said*, can we make a snowman?"

"I'm certainly glad we have you to take care of these things," I cooed sweetly into the phone. "I wouldn't even know who to call. Whom. No, you can't make a snowman because I am going to half *kill* you, and you'll be in the *hospital* till the snow melts."

"What?" said Horace.

"Where are my snowpants?" asked Ben, stepping in

the remains of Vicky's once-neat pile on his way back
to me.

Horace was reminiscing about the blizzard of '67,
when the power was off for three days, and everyone
came to him for water.

"I want my snowpants too," said Matt.

"I'll go *get* them," explained Ben patiently, "if you'll
just tell me where to find them."

I hung up on Horace rather abruptly, though I doubt
if he noticed; he's probably talking still. With the rest of
the snow water I tried to mop up the dog shit and suc-
ceeded only in smearing it, and brought in some more
snow to melt.

"But I want my *snowpants*," said Ben, who has great
powers of concentration. "Me and Matthew are going to
make a snowman."

I carried a candle upstairs and opened the door of my
closet, holding the candle up high in order to get a lot of
hot wax down my neck, like Beauty and the Beast. The
floor of the closet was bulging with grocery bags, some
taped shut and some too full to close at all. I chose one
at random and dragged it out and emptied it on the floor,
and held up the things and peered at them by candle-
light. They seemed to be all underwear with holes in
them. Depressing. I dragged out another bag and dumped
it. Hard to tell what that stuff was. It might have been
dresses Emily used to have, back in first grade when we
wore dresses.

By the time I got down to the snowpants the entire
bedroom floor was deep in ancient clothing, all with that

softened, characterless touch clothes get when they've absolutely given up. It was cold in the bedroom too, and
getting colder. No heat, no water, no light in the house.
Only great toppling mountains of former clothing. A
sea of rags.

The boys went forth to make a snowman.

It was dark in the refrigerator and smelled like a ham-
ster cage, but I found two eggs and boiled them in melted
snow over the fire, and set fire to the pot holder. I ate the
eggs; they were like dinosaur eggs. They could have been
shot from a gun.

Crusted snow dripped reluctantly from my stack of
drying firewood, and the candle flame flickered moodily
in the gray light.

When the power goes back on, if it ever does, I will
have to go upstairs and repack all those clothes into their
wrinkled grocery bags and stow them back in the closet.
By this time next year there will be more bags, and I will
have to put some in my husband's closet. By this time five
years from now . . .

I long for a Japanese sort of existence. Each member
of the family with a grass mat to sleep on, a change of
clothes, a bowl, a cup, a pair of chopsticks. Nothing else.

Think how clean it would be. Think of the twins'
room as it is now, and how everything they touch is destroyed, melts away, King Midas in reverse, and everything they wear ages before your eyes like a flower dying
in a stop-motion film. How their floor is covered with tiny
things too destroyed to identify. Crummy little twisted bits
of plastic and cloth and metal. There is, struggling deep

within my twins, a deep, mysterious, destructive force that I hope to God no one ever harnesses. In the hands of the great world powers it doesn't bear thinking of. They peel the paper off their crayons and the peelings dribble to the floor, and the crayons break into nubbins and fall after them, and drawings taped crookedly on the wall smudge and tatter from the mere presence of my sons, and the wall itself decays.

I have thought of consulting a priest, but it seems easier just to get rid of everything in the house. Somehow.

Maybe we could have a cushion to sit on, one apiece. I will have a single vase with a single rose in it. There will be no closets, no cupboards. Nothing in the kitchen but a hibachi and a bottle of soy sauce. A little charcoal to cook over, a little woodstove for heat.

No flowerpots of perishing avocado plants, stacks of old magazines, cracked saucers. No ragged pajama halves, stained beach towels, half-empty bottles of Caladryl, theater programs from 1963, broken water pistols, shapeless socks, crumpled paper chains for the Christmas tree, photographs of babies, decks of forty-nine playing cards, questionable flashlight batteries, pickle forks, old pocketbooks, three-year-old bank statements, gallon cans containing a quarter of an inch of withered paint, grocery bags full of soggy clothing.

I think wistfully of burning the house down.

OLD CLOTHES CAN BE TREACHEROUS, TOO.

If you put away Ben's jacket in May, and take it out again in October and thrust him into it, and two inches of wrist hang out of the sleeves, then it is clear that Ben has grown and Matt will wear what's left of the jacket this fall. Ben has grown, but he is still the same Ben. It's the clothes that have been in the far, dark back of the closet for years and years that do you in.

The other day I saw, not in a bag but on a little girl in the K-Mart, a coat like the one Emily had the winter she was five, and I started to cry. Tears shattered the road as I drove home.

She wore that coat waiting for the school car, and in the elevator when she came to my office. She was a little girl. There is no other way to look at it: I have lost a little girl. Lost a child. All children are lost; their grow-ing is a continuous process of loss. A tall and handsome Emily occasionally strides around the house now, but the little one, with her wispy pigtails and irrational fits of happiness, is as completely gone as if she had walked into the woods one day and never come back.

While this process is something everyone knows about, and mentions often, it comes as a fresh shock to us all. It is certainly sentimental, and silly, but it is just as certainly true: they were people who have gone away. People you have lost. And twenty years later there you are dishing up the Thanksgiving turkey, and you look around the table at the assembled grownups and their wives and husbands, and you think, yes, but where are my *children?* Where did they *go?*

Driving, in tears, I think: I didn't appreciate her. Didn't pay enough attention. I forgot to notice the last time I stood behind her chair at breakfast and braided her hair for school; the last time I said, "Hold your head still." I was too busy to notice her, those years. Working. Having twins. But surely everyone must think this, even women, if there be such, who had nothing to do while their children grew but lie around drinking margaritas and buffing their nails.

And how much attention, real attention, can anyone pay, for how long? Just a short while ago this road I'm driving down now was a source of pure joy in my life. I used to reel dangerously along this road, staring and staring at the roll of the cornfields and the way that barn is set on the rising swell of the hill. Now I keep my eyes on the pickup truck ahead of me, wishing it would get a move on and wondering what to have for dinner. You can't just keep staring at a child, either, as it grows, and seeing it all the time. All you can really do is remember. The present zips by pretty quickly, but the past hangs around. You see it better backward; you can see them, all of them, the children they were every winter and summer, in the different coats and bathing suits they wore, and watch them all walk into the woods and never come back.

CHAPTER FIVE

A person who has earned and saved up ninety-three dollars and bought herself a pony may still be technically a child, but is no longer someone whose coat you button, whose hair you braid.

It was the week before school started. We had been officially resident in the country for two summers and a winter, and I had learned the shortest route to the liquor store and the supermarket, and whom to call when the septic tank overflowed or a tree blew down across the driveway or all the tiles in the children's bathroom fell into the tub and broke. I drove swiftly and accurately along our crooked narrow roads, and blew my horn at the timid. I braked for pheasants and groundhogs, and slowed down for horses.

We were on our way with the twins for their ceremonial pre-school haircut. (The barber is Kristin's father. The man who unloads the septic tank is Billy's father. The man who stuck the tiles back is Bridget and Chrissy's uncle. This is the country; there are no strangers. Except, of course, us. We will always be strangers. On the old deed maps of the township our name, even in variant spelling, does not appear.)

On this particular occasion I rounded a nasty curve and slammed on the brakes for a pride of ponies. A tall college-age girl was riding one of them, with her legs dangling, and the rest followed. All the ponies wore the demurely satisfied expression I was to come to recognize as the look of a pony who has escaped, escaping being the true end and purpose of a pony's life, and enjoyed a jaunt, and has now been captured and is being taken home. Ponies, unlike horses, are bright and easily bored. Escape, travel, evasion, capture, and return are a pony's novel, its television, conversation, movies, theater, and ballet.

I didn't know this at the time. I did soon.

I came to a full stop, since the ponies were using up the road, and Emily leaned waist-deep out the window and hailed the girl, who seemed to have been a teacher at the riding school.

"Hello, Emily," said the girl. "Say, did you ever get yourself a pony?"

At this point, if I had had my wits about me, I would have thrust the gas pedal to the floor and driven straight into them.

"No," said Emily, "but I have ninety-three dollars in the bank."

The girl turned around and looked morosely at the pony behind her. "Dewdrop is for sale," she said.

" 'Dewdrop'?" I said.

Dewdrop batted her blond eyelashes. She was a

glamorous little thing with a face like a bad pansy, a dappled chocolate brown with ash-blond mane, tail, and eyelashes.

"Is ninety-three dollars enough?" asked Emily.

"NO," I said. "Absolutely not. Emily, we don't have any place to keep it. I can't—"

"Well, I was asking two hundred and fifty," said the girl.

"Good," I said. "I'm sure that's a fair price."

"But a good home is the most important thing."

"Oh, I'm *sure* you can get two-fifty for her. After all—"

"You mean I can have her for ninety-three dollars?"

"But, Emily, where would we—"

"Besides, my father says if I'm away at college, and he's got three ponies and two horses to take care of, and nobody riding them, and I've got to sell *somebody*."

"But Emily—"

"Can I come and get her tomorrow?"

"On the porch, it could live," said Matthew.

The next morning we went to the bank and drew out Emily's ninety-three dollars.

"I guess this is pony day, huh?" said the bank teller, and Emily smiled back at her. (The country again. The bank tellers know the destiny of every dollar you hand them; the man at the Sunoco station knows about the slow leak in my right front; the checkout girl at the supermarket knows the twins can't have any gum.)

My husband dropped the four of us off at the girl's farm and drove quickly away. We all took turns riding Dewdrop home. It was one of those days with a cobalt sky a thousand miles high, and the ditches shouting with crickets and foaming with Queen Anne's lace. We had borrowed a bridle, but there was no saddle, and Dewdrop's muscles moved warmly between the thighs. She glanced alertly from side to side. She was young, and born on the farm where we got her, and had never spent a night away from home.

It was three miles, and we each got several turns. As we moved majestically down our own lane, even I felt a twinge of triumph. We passed the houses of our children's friends and enemies, picking up a following of kids as we proceeded, and bowed and smiled to the populace like royalty. Or, perhaps, looking more like Mary on her way to Bethlehem.

It was Emily's eleventh birthday.

We unwrapped a lot of clothesline from the chairs in the boys' room and fastened Dewdrop to the maple tree. All the kids from the neighborhood climbed on and off her, and fed her with chunks of lawn pulled up by the roots. Emily brushed her mane and tail with my hairbrush. Dewdrop seemed pleased.

Then it was lunch time. The neighborhood kids went home, and the four of us went inside to make sandwiches.

The minute the screen door banged behind our backs, Dewdrop broke the clothesline and started up the road the way she came. Briskly.

Emily and I ran after her, and caught her halfway up the lane, and I learned that you do not chase a pony, you have to surround it. Even if there's only one of you, you have to surround it. We brought her back and knotted the clothesline together and tied her up again, and Emily sat on her to eat her sandwich. Dewdrop seemed content.

When Emily had to come inside to go to the bathroom, Dewdrop broke the clothesline and started back up the road the way she came.

The fourth time she broke the clothesline, she got clear up to the place where we cut our Christmas tree, and I had to get help from neighbors with cars.

I called the mother of a friend of the boys'. She lives in an old house down on the highway, with an old barn, one of those barns with the cone-shaped pillars that I like so much, and rides with the Kimberton Hunt. Dewdrop, she said a little doubtfully, was welcome there, but only temporarily. Because of her tendency to acquire horses and ponies, her husband had gotten quite paranoid, and kept going out to the barn to count them.

We took Dewdrop down there and secured her behind the ancient, solid stones of their barnyard wall, and left her inspecting it for cracks and weaknesses.

The next day, a friend of Emily's called. She lives around the block from us (the distance around the block is just under four miles) on half-a-hundred acres, and owns an enormous placid-looking bay horse with feet like manhole covers and a mildly retarded expression. Dewdrop could come and stay there for a while, and Emily could ride with her friend Barby.

I am relieved; maybe this pony business won't be quite so difficult and alarming after all. Barby's parents, who probably know what they're doing, will be responsible for

the wretched thing, not I. On the whole, I rather think I
won't get Matthew that cow.

We chivy the pony around a lot of lanes and byways
and blackberry prickles, to avoid hacking down the highway, and warp her across a creek and up the hill to Barby's
stable, and introduce her to the horse. The horse looks
askance.

Dewdrop's stall is not ready for her, being full of loose
rocks and empty sacks and bits of rope and broken lad-
ders and such odds and ends as people keep in empty
stalls, so Dewdrop is put into the field while Emily cleans
out the stall.

I go home to figure out what to have for dinner. At
sunset, I drive back to fetch Emily and meet, on the way,
Barby's parents driving in all directions in several cars
looking for Dewdrop. The fence that easily contained the
enormous retarded-looking horse has been a source of
amused contempt for a pony. I join the search, driving
around and around the darkening lanes peering through
the windshield for a blond tail. I have a vision of the years
to come, driving around country lanes with a rope and a
carrot in the glove compartment, a vision that subsequent-
ly comes to pass, except that after a while I stop using the
car and go on foot, so as not to have to walk back for
the car.

I go to Dewdrop's old home and inquire there, but she
has not been seen, so I leave my phone number and drive
on. At moonrise, I return to Barby's place, and Dewdrop
has been found; a friendly farmer had stuck her in with
his cows. I leave Emily still wearily heaving debris out of

the stall while Dewdrop, tied with heavy rope to a bolt in the aisle, watches with cheerful interest. At 10 P.M. Emily comes home in Barby's clothes, with her own oozing mud in a garbage bag, and drops into bed.

The next day school starts, and the boys, grousing, enter first grade. Leaving me a free woman. Free to drive to the tack shop and buy not one but two canvas-webbing stall doors, so the pony can neither climb over nor crawl under.

She immediately does both, and throws all the tack on the floor and stomps on it, gets into the oats, breaks a riding crop, takes off her halter and buries it somewhere, rips up a length of fence, and vanishes into the great world again. And is again found and brought back, looking demurely satisfied.

THERE ARE TWO FIRST GRADES IN OUR SCHOOL AND THE boys have been separated, one in each. Matthew seems pleased to be separated. Ben is rather miffed, and rummages through Matt's papers, grumbling, after school.

Emily is now in a different school, an ancient building in Downingtown where the radiators creak and whistle, and takes the early school bus at seven-ten, fastidiously holding her nose; the big kids smoke raw, choky, homegrown pot in the back. The boys take the late bus, at eight twenty-five. Both stop at our corner. The neighborhood gathers there, with much banter and bashing of schoolbags and lunches, lots of dogs on hand to cheer them off. The bus collects them and groans up the hill and disappears beyond the trees. The dogs go back to their respective homes, pausing only to tip over our garbage cans and sort the contents.

It gets pretty quiet around here. Boy and I are together. I talk to him, and he answers, and blinks at me with love in his gold eyes; he has waited so long.

My husband and I go to Parents' Night, and separate into the two first grade rooms.

I walk around Matthew's room looking politely at the drawings on the walls. At the huge poster of Ella the Elephant, whose trunk daily selects a peanut with a child's name on it. (To what end? For what sinister purpose is this child-of-the-day elected?) The rest of the wall space is covered with lists. There are two sets of lists; one, a brief one, is headed What Mommy Does All Day. Mommy cooks, irons curtains (*Irons curtains?* Fleeting impression of Russian diplomacy in the home.), makes cookies, takes care of baby, goes to the store. That's about all. The second list, on half a dozen sheets of drawing paper, covers an entire wall and is headed What Daddy Does All Day. Now, in the city Daddy's work would make pretty tame reading, but this isn't the city, and Daddy drives the tractor, mows the field, plants corn, cuts down trees with chain saw, mixes cement, drives a truck, builds houses, slaughters pigs, goes hunting, and has a perfectly rip-roaring time. If I were a girl child in this class I would open my wrists. It must be fairly mystifying to Matthew, too, whose mommy plants corn and mows the field and whose daddy merely vanishes boringly into a commuter train. No, I guess it's not mystifying. As I remember, people accept what they learn in school. When reality conflicts with education, at six, education wins every time. No doubt when he comes home from school to find mommy cutting up the broken cherry tree with a chain saw, his vision blurs, and superimposed on the sight of me is another, realer me, making cookies.

Matthew's teacher calls me at home. I freeze, and simper tensely, but it's all right; she only wants me to come in and talk to the class. They are studying what mommies and daddies do, and selected specimens are to come in and talk. If I would do so, bringing with me some of the tools I use in my work . . .

Of course I would. I would be delighted. I won't, I say, drag in my precious typewriter, but I would be happy to talk about advertising, copywriting, and various ways to scratch up money with the written word.

There is a pause. A long, long pause, and finally I say, "Hello?"

She clears her throat. "No," she says firmly. "No, that isn't what I mean. We're studying what *mommies* do right now. If you could bring in, oh, say, your steam iron, or an electric mixer, and talk about using them . . ."

I wonder where the iron is. I used to have one, but I don't think it survived the move from town. "But I want to talk about advertising," I say.

"No. That would come under Daddies and the Larger Community. We don't start that till January."

In spite of the evidence of the lists, I can hardly believe it, and instead of being horrified I am rather impressed. It seems downright brave of this woman, at this time in the world, to be able to say such a thing, let alone teach it to twenty-three six-year-olds. Kind of schizo, though. After all, this woman works. Teaching first grade is not the same thing as ironing curtains.

However, I feel I owe something to the girl children in my son's class. "Call me in January," I say. "I will come in with the daddies. I will come in and talk about advertising."

"Yes. Yes, certainly."

"Don't forget. *Call me.*"

I never hear from her again, of course. I am irrelevant. Outside the course of study.

The city seems very far away, and for a while I can't decide whether it is we out here who are remote from things, or perhaps we *are* the things, and it's the city that's remote, cut off over there.

In either case i'm a liar. a housewife is what i am, not a copywriter, and a terrible housewife too. Here I am with all my children in school and no job, no excuse, and look at the place.

The kitchen is infested with ants. The books are covered with cobwebs and mildew, the children's bathroom is covered with toothpaste and worse, the flat surfaces everywhere are furred with dust and mapped with the aimless tracks of dried spilled tea, and covered with torn homework papers, and mateless gloves, and old magazines, and junk mail urging me to send in my lucky number and win things. A cat has been sick on the floor. In the laundry room, mountains of clean laundry waiting to be folded have toppled and mingled with the mountains of dirty

laundry waiting to be washed, so I will have to separate
it, inspecting it under a strong light, sniffing it, as if it
really mattered. I mean, if it's that hard to tell, what difference does it make? I suppose it does make a difference,
though. It must. If I accidentally put an unwashed towel
back in the linen closet among the clean ones, something
has come loose. We have taken a long slide down the hill
toward slovenry. I have to hang on, halfway down. Dig
my fingers in. Spray something on the ants, though I hate
to use poison in the kitchen, feeling superstitiously that
it will somehow lurk there and, when my back is turned,
leap into the Cheerios. I must do something, with my
thumbnail, about the toothpaste on the bathroom wall. I
must scrabble around on this slippery, greasy slope trying to gain a few inches before we slip back any further.
The house plants are white with dust. Something dark and
sticky has been spilled in the refrigerator and seeped down
under the vegetable drawers. The window by the stove is
so gray that every day looks cloudy. The breadbox smells
of mold and the cats have fleas and there's nothing for
dinner. Some chicken in the freezer, I think, but the children have warmly informed me that they will leave home
in a body the next time they see chicken, disguise it how I
may. The neighbor's dog has spread the garbage the whole
length of the driveway, which is silly, since meat scraps
around here are scarce as penguins and the best he could
do is a butter wrapper, or a sardine can pre-licked by cats.
We're out of milk and matches and mustard and there's no
toilet paper in the downstairs bathroom and there's jelly
on the wall by the breakfast table and I am not holding

my own. I am slipping. Every day. There is a point, close to the bottom, from which there is no climbing back, not even with professional help, and I can see it rising up to meet me, in quick little slips and rushes.

There are two cereal bowls on the kitchen floor. The dog is supposed to clean them up, but sometimes rebels. Rice Krispies have dried tightly to their sides. Have you ever noticed how fiercely Rice Krispies cling to things? What can they possibly be *made* of?

I am haunted by visions of decent order. A pot of daisies on a scrubbed and polished table, with sunlight shining in through invisible window glass, sweet-smelling curtains, *ironed* curtains, stirring in the breeze. A bureau drawer in which all the undershirts are folded, and each sock rolled together with a matching sock.

Someone has spilled sugar on the floor, and in guiltily trying to wipe it up has spread it into the four corners and tracked a lot into the living room.

Damned ants.

How do people manage?

The other night I was sitting in a neighbor's living room, and I dropped a Cheese Bit. It bounced and rolled under my chair, the way Cheese Bits do, and I went burrowing after it.

It was clean under the chair. The floor was polished, and the baseboard under there was clean, and the edge of the rug, which exerts an electrical attraction for woozies, was woozyless. The only foreign body under there was my Cheese Bit, which I retrieved and ate. I'd hate to eat a Cheese Bit that got under a chair in *my* house.

How does she do it?

As a sort of solution to the problem, I go out and buy a peck of green beans for the freezer, and spend the rest of the day on a stool in the kitchen by a pot of boiling water, watching the clock while they blanch, in batches. I drain them, chill them, dry them, pack them in plastic bags, and put them in the freezer, where they will remain, perhaps forever.

This makes me feel better. I am a *good* housewife; see me providently freezing beans against the barren winter? For two cents I'd make jelly.

None of this activity has any affect on the ants, or the toothpaste, or the laundry.

There is janitorial housewifery and creative housewifery, and the creative is kind of fun but strictly optional these days, and if you do a lot of it you won't have any time for the janitorial part, which is not fun, or optional either.

A strong smell of reheated horse leaks into the living room from something of Emily's left by the door. Her boots, or jacket. A broken bridle dangles from one of the dining room chairs. I'm supposed to do something about it. Take it to be mended, or give it back to its rightful owner or something, but I don't.

That broken bridle does a lot for the room.

People whose living rooms smell of horse, whose chairs wear broken bridles, have more important things to do than scrape toothpaste. Such people are basically farmers, not janitors, and in the summer they are busy in the fields, and in the fall there's all that canning and preserving, and probably a hog to slaughter and sausage to make, and in the winter they have broken bridles to mend and stock to take care of, and then there's spring planting. For such people a house is a shelter from the weather, a workshop, not a trinket to wash and polish and show off. You can't expect such people to do anything about the state of the oven, in spite of the way it smokes now at speeds over 350°, or clean the ventilator over the stove.

All of this is a lie and I know it, but I leave the broken bridle there anyway, in case of unexpected visitors.

In the course of time the living arrangements for the pony came unstuck, as all arrangements will, and there was the pony again, her sweet face poked inquiringly in at the laundry room door, her eye on the refrigerator whence carrots come. Once, when I was off at the grocery store trying to decide what to have for dinner, Emily rode her in through the laundry room door, and the kitchen, and the parlor, and out through the sliding doors, and ever since she's been trying to get back in. Like the dog, she feels she is house people, a creature of carpets and couches.

My husband was firm about her living in the house, but she had to live somewhere.

Here and there in our woods, overgrown and nailed down with vines, half visible under blackberries and poison ivy, were various piles of old boards in an advanced state of decomposition, bristling with rusty nails, and also several rolls of wire fencing. I found a place where the trees had grown conveniently into a lopsided oval, and could have a fence attached to them. I bought a box of enormous staples, and a wire-cutter. Bleeding from black-berry scratches, I dragged the rolls of fencing out of their weeds and fastened the stuff to the oval of trees. It looked like something the twins would make. In the places where the trees were too far apart, I dug holes and planted crooked chunks of firewood and wispy saplings to serve as fence posts.

Between two of the trees Emily and I set a young hick-ory tree for a ridge pole, and slanted two more down to the ground. These we filled in with our collection of rotten boards to make a lean-to, and covered its three sides with roofing paper. The effect suggested a tent thrown up by a troop of drunken Boy Scouts in a hurricane.

For a gate, I screwed brackets into two other trees, and laid two-by-fours across them. Boy sat on a rock at a safe distance and watched me.

The whole project took up most of that fall, and was quite amazingly hard work. I groaned, getting out of bed in the morning, and rubbed various places. It was, how-ever, the kind of honest labor that separates us farmers from the housewives, and excuses us from making beds.

My husband complained that the pen was too close to the road. He said it was an eyesore, and I didn't speak to him for three days.

Into this elaborate and rickety cage we put Dewdrop, and if she laughed, I didn't hear her. No doubt she smiled quietly.

Emily and I drove to the feed-and-grain mill to buy three bales of hay, which was all I could fit in the car. There is something very *authentic* about going to the mill for hay. I found myself swaggering a little. I considered spitting on the floor. On the way home I drove with a reckless dash and carelessness, one finger on the wheel, one arm dangling out the window. I just might get that cow after all. The car smelled lovely, like fields.

Dewdrop had removed the two-by-fours from their brackets and left.

She left by the gate, she left by the fence, she went under the fence, she went through the fence, she leaned on the fence till it buckled and my clumsy fence posts fell and she walked *over* the fence. The clerks in the hardware store got so they laughed automatically when I came in. I scowled at them, and bought more latches, braces, staples, brackets.

Sociable Dewdrop was lonely in our woods. She had struck up a friendship with Barby's horse; horses and ponies are subject to deep, silent, complicated relationships with each other, and she missed Barby's horse. While Emily was in school she missed Emily. Every twenty minutes or so I would drop what I was doing and go up to see her. If she was still there I would throw her some more hay. I kept hoping hay would keep her entertained, tossing it around, and peeing in it, and so on. She would eat a mouthful, and look up at me dangerously with her pansy eyes: *Stay and talk to me. If you go back in the house I will leave.*

But I have things to do in the house.

Stay and talk to me.

I got so I recognized the look in her eye when she was planning to leave.

I bought a roll of the best German barbed wire. My husband said it was left over from Auschwitz, and refused to help me with it, and it weighed a ton. Besides being, of course, prickly. I felt bad about using it; I could see our lovely pony ripped and bleeding; but I was desperate. Outside of and among the rusty fencing, using another whole box of staples, I ran four strands of bright new tight shining bristly barbed wire, tearing my jacket on barbs and pounding staples into my thumb and swearing horribly. Dewdrop, inside, followed me and watched. Her warm breath ruffled my hair. She peered so closely at my project that there was no room to swing the hammer without hitting her velvet nose.

I finished and straightened up, rubbing my back, and she looked me in the eye: *Stay and talk to me.*

Huh. Let's see you get out of *that.*

Swinging my hammer, I strolled back to the house. Ten minutes later, from the bathroom window, I watched her moving across the pen in that purposeful, head-down way. She kept on walking. She did not duck, or dig, or lean, or wriggle; she just walked, and I watched, and thought, But the pen doesn't *go* that far, does it? It can't.

I didn't believe it until she was actually across the stream and headed for the hill behind the neighbors'.

Even before I went for the carrot and the rope, I wasted precious minutes checking the pen to see what had happened.

The shiny barbed wire was still tightly in place, except for a section of the lowest strand, six inches from the ground; it was loose from one tree. And yet I had seen her. I had watched her walk through that very place without hesitating, without breaking stride.

Was she magic? Or was she bleeding to death somewhere?

It took three hours to find her, that time. The Millers were keeping her in their barnyard, and she leaned over the fence demurely and whickered at me. I searched her all over. Nowhere on her strong glossy hide was there the smallest scratch. I grabbed her by the forelock and stared into the purple depths of her brown eyes. Was she a witch? She tossed her head and nibbled at my coat sleeve, happy to see me, a little reproachful this time: *What took you so long? I waited and waited.*

Of course she was a witch. All ponies are witches.

IN THE MEANTIME, AS IF I DIDN'T HAVE ENOUGH TO DO, I fetched up with a solid crack against the social structure of the county.

I had wondered from the beginning how they were going to fit us in, since we didn't hunt anything except sometimes, futilely, missing domestic objects like the Phillips screwdriver and Ben's spelling book. It turned out that hunting wasn't the primary factor at all but only a visible symptom, like spots, of the basic matter.

It turned out to be done with houses. Not with their size or splendor; heavens, no; an enormous house means only that you have money, which is vulgar and has nothing to do with being rich. If you have money, chances are you've worked for it, you poor toad. The rich may have jobs, and even show up at them occasionally, but their jobs are curiously unconnected to their income. Income is something else, remote, elusive, and pure. Unsmeared by the hand of labor. I think the Tooth Fairy leaves it under their pillow. The world of invested capital and inherited land is as mysterious to me as Oz.

Very few of the rich here have money. What they have is the right house.

The right house was built of stone in the eighteenth or early nineteenth century and has a large barn of the same period. The bottom of the barn is stone and the top is wood. Around these structures are fields with thorough-breds in them, enclosed by fence. Post-and-rail fence. This is, as they say in the real estate ads, hunt country, and heaven help the pighead who would put up wire fence. I suppose the Master of Foxhounds carries wireclippers just in case, and on their way through your vegetable garden and living room the hunt lays a curse on you; your lawn withers, your children waste away, your dog dies in fits, and the roof falls in. The hunt has the right-of-way.

It helps to have inherited the right house rather than just bought it. If the place you live in has been known as the Hatfield place for two hundred years, it's as well to be named Hatfield. (The house *should* be known as the Hatfield place. It is not good form, not rich, to call it Happy Acres or Foxview. Only twentieth-century ranch houses are called Foxview.)

If you have a barn and fields, your children have ponies and you ride to hounds.

If you have no barn because it burned down in

1881, or because your house was the old grist mill or George Washington's fever hospital, then you walk to bassets.

To an outsider, the rich might be confused with the farmers, who live in old houses too, but the distinction here is simple: farmers have ugly blue aluminum silos and a corn crib, and big angry-looking machinery standing around their front yards like dinosaurs frozen in the act of extinction. A farmer's work is connected to his income. Farmers do not ride to hounds or walk to bassets; farmers shoot deer.

If you live in a twentieth-century house with no barn, I believe you're allowed to go fishing.

It is not a fluid society. You stay in your place. If you live in the wrong house, no grace of mind or person, nor wit nor fame nor civic effort nor private virtue shall lead you across that gulf.

Our house was built in 1961, and no amount of stone facing can conceal that abject fact. Also our land is woods, not fields. Beautiful ancient woods, full of complex and towering beeches, gum trees that turn scarlet on Labor Day, red newts under stones, and round clear little springs you can drink from, but woods nevertheless. I used to like it. As Dewdrop settled in with us, and Emily twice a day carried her gallon milk bottles of water up the hill to the pony pen, I began to see it all for what it was. Unrich. A rural slum.

We had no barn. We had a tangle of wires and a crooked lean-to that, on rare and favored occasions, loosely contained a pony.

I suppose I was almost expecting it by the time the SPCA called.

They had had complaints from a neighbor of ours. We had a pony, and neither barn nor field.

I'm fond of the SPCA, and I was polite even when he kept referring to Dewdrop as abused and neglected. I said I thought there must be some mistake.

No. There was no mistake. Our neighbor had been perfectly clear about it, and extremely upset, too.

Like a light bulb exploding, I knew who the neighbor was; I had seen him stop his car and inspect our haphazard construction, but like an ass I'd thought he was admiring the pony. I knew where the neighbor lived. It was one of the most charming of the really old houses, in a county where eighteenth-century goes in to dinner before nineteenth.

I asked what I was expected to do.

The SPCA man was having trouble keeping his temper. Obviously, he said, I would have to get a barn. Immediately. Otherwise they would be forced to have the pony mercifully destroyed.

Now, the connection between a barn and a pony is purely social. Ponies don't go *in* barns, and no one expects them to; you see them all around here, all winter long, blanketed only in sleet; ponies don't get cold, they get claustrophobia. Anyone who's read up on the climate of the Shetland Isles knows it isn't easy to freeze a pony. What we had done was violate the essential fitness of things, like an anarchist lunching in the Union League, or a cat barking.

I spent several days pacing around the pony pen wringing my hands, followed by the delighted Dewdrop. It would take months, and thousands, just to clear the land. Bring in fill. Lay a foundation. I had no money and, as it turned out, no time.

All that work wasted. I began to call around looking for another charitable home for our big awkward child.

The SPCA arrived in person. He was a puffing, furious little man, and we conferred in the driveway.

My poor neighbor, he said, was on the phone to them day and night, half distracted with worry. And here I had *deliberately*, arrogantly defied their kind warning. Now something had to be done at once to put the poor creature out of its suffering. (Alas, he meant the pony, not the neighbor.)

It was a mild and cloudy day, and Dewdrop, munching, regarded us over the fence and offered to shake hands for a carrot. She was wearing her new blue coat, and *I* thought she looked pretty spiffy, but the SPCA man stood with his back to her, shouting and waving his arms.

"Ponies left out in the open like that," he said, "become infested with lice!"

This stopped me; my jaw dropped. "Honest?" I said. "I don't understand. *Lice?* How?"

He pushed his face into mine and shouted, spraying spit, "From neglect!" Then, controlling himself, he went on more kindly, "You see, people like you, people who don't understand anything about horses, don't know these things."

He looked past me, over my shoulder, at my house.

Built in 1961. Barnless. I cringed. Of course I didn't know anything about horses. What could I know? Women in houses like ours are housewives; they know how to get their husbands' shirt collars clean. Women with barns, who ride to hounds, know instinctively what to do for founder and galls. And lice.

The children of houses like ours have cars, not ponies. We know a fourteen-year-old who's already on his second car, and a ten-year-old recently confided in me that he wouldn't mind having a VW, just until he got his license. They have fleets, flotillas of motorcycles, snowmobiles, trail bikes, and, for the under-six set, riding mowers, but only the children of houses with barns have ponies, and the ponies stand with their tails to the blizzard, dreaming of the Shetland Isles.

The SPCA man told me it was for the good of everyone concerned, and he would be back in an hour with a warrant and a truck.

I did the only thing I could think of at the moment. I turned my back on him and with furiously trembling hands managed to get Dewdrop's bridle on, poking her ears roughly through the brow band, and then I scrambled up onto her warm fat back, with all the grace and dignity of anyone climbing onto a saddleless pony. I rode away.

As a triumphant gesture it was pretty pathetic, but it felt better than bursting into tears. I was shaking hard with rage, and I suppose what I looked like was a housewife in a thrift-shop jacket with my legs dangling down from a Shetland pony, but I sat up very straight and felt, briefly, rich and scornful.

I hoped the SPCA man would come bumbling after me, afoot like a peasant, but he didn't.

I had no idea where to go, so I headed for the temporary shelter where we took her the first day, after she kept breaking clotheslines. She would be safe there for the moment, anyway. We went down the lane, and through the woods, and across the highway, and up to the house. I dismounted, turning my ankle, and knocked on the door, hoping for sympathy, and an angry chat and a cup of coffee.

There was no one home.

I stood for a while holding Dewdrop with my nose running. I couldn't take her home again. I didn't know anywhere else to take her, and I couldn't just keep standing there, so finally I turned her into the barnyard anyway; I could call later and explain.

As I left, Dewdrop ran back and forth on the other side of the stone walk whinnying after me. Even witches get attached to their homes and people.

I walked back up the lane. Back in my proper place again, a housewife, on foot. It was a long walk and it started to rain.

The SPCA man was gone.

Some days later I go out by the lane to plant daffodil bulbs. A neighbor, a different neighbor, passes by in a pickup truck with a horse-trailer. He is wearing his red coat and his black velvet hard hat and he is not, of course, driving the pickup truck. You can't get dressed up in all that stuff and drive a truck. A man is driving it, a plain man. He probably doesn't even have a name.

I have met this neighbor at various functions and events, but he doesn't remember. He doesn't glance at me, out there grubbing among the bulbs; his profile does not waver in my direction; it would be wrong of him to notice, although probably he senses me instinctively as a kind of cancer growing on the landscape. I see, in the trailer, the behinds of two horses wearing white lace dressing gowns. Some of the horses around here have more clothes than I do. They turn the corner at the end of the lane and disappear, headed for the meet.

I feel dirty and small, irrelevant, toad-shaped, unworthy. Shall I climb into a hole with the bulbs and scrape dirt over my head?

Presently the hunt my neighbor rides with will spread this way, and at the crossings of every country lane a brace of girls will appear to hold up traffic, in case the hunt wants to use the lane. These girls are tall and narrow, with serious narrow blond faces and their pale hair coiled up under their hard hats, and they sit on very tall horses that stand at attention. Their boots glisten. I think if they smile, even at each other, they get drummed out of the hunt, but I don't know; it's never happened. If you try to pass, they hold out an arm or a riding crop, but avoid eye contact. Her Majesty's household guards are a pack of clowns compared to these kids.

I leave the daffodil bulbs on the ground and go back to the house, trying not to slink.

Maybe I should cancel the pond.

I've been wanting a pond ever since we came. There's a place on our stream that's perfect to be dammed, and there'd be a little rowboat for the kids to fall out of and maybe a couple of ducks, and now I've finally gathered up the money and called the bulldozer man. But I don't know.

Is it all right? Or not? Looking around, I see that the rich have ponds and people like us have swimming pools. The only unrich with ponds are the farmers, and farmers have special privileges, on account of preserving what we call in zoning meetings "the essentially rural nature of the area." *Can* people like us have ponds?

There's no way to find out. I can scarcely go around from door to massive stone-girt door, knocking, tugging my forelock, saying, "Please, sir, may I have a pond?" They wouldn't answer. Nobody's going to tell me the rules. I just have to wait and find out. It may be that when it's all finished, and the bulldozer man paid off, and the ducks installed, the rich will come trotting over the bridge in their pony carts, and pause, and all of them together will somehow just know it won't do. Won't do at all. Then the authorities will take note and come around, and the pond will develop a sinister new aspect in their eyes. Death trap. Cesspool. It will have to be dynamited and drained at great expense.

Paranoia blossoms like a flower in the brain. I am filled with vague images of the sans-culottes, the howling torchlit mob at the gates, uprisings of serfs and peasantry throughout the ages. I can feel myself growing fangs.

The first thing to do is get us organized. In union there is strength. Nothing to lose but our chains. It will be seen, when we all gather, at the Rollerama probably, that subtle changes have overtaken this once-respectable though unrich population. Our gait is shambling, our speech a surly mumble. All it takes is a few well-chosen words, a shouted slogan, and we are on our feet, howling, infested with lice, brandishing clubs . . .

I'm not precisely sure what happens next, but you'll see the pictures in the papers. That'll be me, the one with the flaming torch and the fangs, third from the right.

WHEN THE GROUND THAWS, I HAVE THE POND DUG AND dammed, and wait nervously. The rich rein in on the bridge, horses dancing with impatience, and look at the rising waters and try to decide.

Apparently it's all right. The crucial weeks pass by, and then the pond becomes an established fact, part of the landscape, and I begin to relax.

Dewdrop never comes home to live with us again, and the rich fade back out of our lives.

DEWDROP LIVES WITH A SERIES OF TOLERANT PEOPLE. I feel bad about it, as if I had rejected a child of my own, and turned it away to live on the sufferance of strangers, but Dewdrop is happy. She has other horses, other ponies. On frosty nights they stand together in the fields, dark shapes under the stars, and think the same thoughts. In August they stand head to tail under a tree brushing the flies from each other's faces, quieted by their secret communion. She takes off only occasionally now, when the faraway hills call to her too strongly.

The following summer the twins peel the boards off

the lean-to to build a fort, and the fort collapses, and the boards rot quietly under vines and blackberries, where they were to start with. Dogwood seedlings grow up in the fenced enclosure.

Emily smells strongly of horse.

A girl with a pony is genderless. She is as far as she will ever get from housewifery. She and Dewdrop go pounding up the hillside together, Emily's long hair leaping behind her, and the pony indulges in a buck and flourish of heels, and Emily's delighted laugh ruffles backward on the wind. It is hard to imagine her folding laundry, or spooning cereal into a baby and scraping the overflow off its chin.

I find I am willing to pay for things like saddle soap and salt blocks, and to do a lot of driving and a lot of standing around on windy hilltops with my eyes tearing and the spaghetti sauce burning at home, waiting. I like to watch her canter away over the hill, as if she was free, and could ride for a long, long way, as far as she wanted, singing loudly, all her life.

In tack shops and feed-and-grain mills and at horse shows in the blazing sun or icy drizzle, I see other mothers. I am sure that they, like me, have other things to do, but here they are, here we all are, offering up our time and patience to our daughters on horseback. I expect we are all thinking the same thing; probably there is the same complicated look in all our eyes.

CHAPTER SIX

When I am not wrestling with bales of hay and sacks of Horse Chows, or standing around waiting for Emily to finish mucking out, I do all those other things.

I wash the hairbrushes and pick up the boys after softball and tie up bundles of newspapers with string and call the man about the drier and wash sweaters and take the dog for her rabies shot and mop the kitchen floor again and make beds and fold laundry and scrape dishes into a garbage bag and remember to buy tomato seedlings, string, duct tape, shelf paper, nose drops, hay, milk, peanut butter, Baggies, scotch, stamps, dishwasher soap, socks, lemons, aspirin, and some more corn meal to mix with water for Ben's orphan baby rabbits, still miraculously alive in their shoe box every morning.

From time to time, waiting in the checkout line or on the phone to make a doctor's appointment for Matt, I think about working, and how simple it was. How I did only one thing, one kind of thing, all day; or at least, how everything I did was bent to a single purpose, and when it was done it stayed done. Such a day makes the head feel peaceful and spacious inside, and strong. Effective. The head addresses itself to its task, accomplishes it, and lo, the task lies down, accomplished, and does not spring back up at you the minute you take your hand off.

A housewife never accomplishes anything. The dishes scraped after dinner last night must be scraped again after lunch. The boys must be picked up *again* after softball. The damp towels harvested from the bathroom floor will be on the bathroom floor again tomorrow, and again the next day. The mind of the housewife never gets to feel triumphant, since nothing is ever done, no problem ever stays conquered, except over such long periods of time, as in toilet-training a child, that there never comes that sharp victorious moment when a thing is visibly accomplished.

I think it damages the brain, never to feel itself as an effective instrument. I think it is bad for it to be splintered, daily, into a thousand unrelated bits and flung off in all directions, but uselessly, like a barrage of rubber arrows. It lives in a constant state of impotence, helplessness against problems, total futility. At the end of the working day nothing has been done that will not have to be done over, and it was hard work, too. You spend the afternoon planning and making dinner, and people eat it in four and a half minutes, and you spend the evening cleaning up after it, and tomorrow you will have to do it again. The obvious inference is that you must be doing it *wrong*.

All this futile effort makes the housewife feel incompetent, and presently she becomes timid and ineffective in her dealings with the world: how could I possibly take

Emily to New York for a matinee? How would I get the tickets? Find the theater? Find New York? I've read about a nervous illness, peculiar to housewives, in which they grow afraid to travel any farther than the supermarket, and then afraid even to leave the house, and finally won't come out from under the bed.

We try to tell ourselves that all this repetitive, ceaseless activity is necessary to the survival of our families, but it isn't, really. Oh, I suppose they'd starve if they weren't fed, or at least if there weren't food around for them to eat, but no one would perish if I never, never picked up the wet towels in the bathroom. The towels would mildew, and stink, and presently there would be no more clean ones in the linen closet, and people would use the mildewy ones, or just stand there until their skin dried. Only, somehow, I have to pick them up *anyway*. I don't know of any woman with the courage or curiosity to try never doing any housework at all except that minimum essential to survival. I wonder what would happen.

A housewife is a person who does, in private, all day, what apparently someone must do, and never gets anything done.

As soon as I get home, and put the groceries away on shelves and in the refrigerator, and put the shampoo on the bottom step to be carried upstairs someday, I take the bow saw and go out and cut down a maple that's been shading the vegetable garden.

It feels lovely. The tree sways, trembles, and falls, and lies there waiting to become firewood. It will not have to be cut down again tomorrow. I have done something, and the peaceful, triumphant spot in the brain feels so real I could touch it.

Then it's time to decide what to make for dinner.

FUTILE AND REPETITIOUS THOUGH IT MAY BE, HOUSE-wifery does have the advantage of reality. It is a primary occupation, dealing with real people and genuine objects and occurrences. Most public occupations are secondary or worse; they do not touch directly on anything of prime reality. After you've been a housewife for a few years, the shop talk of people with public jobs, unless their shop is farming or surgery or collecting garbage, has an eerie quality of make-believe about it. How can they possibly take it seriously? It's so remote, a game, figures changing on a board, pieces of paper changing hands. People who live too long in this abstract public shadow-world get to thinking it's real. They live among such make-believe, and deal with so many things that not only don't matter but can scarcely be said to exist at all in any concrete sense, that they can't feel what's under their own hands. It turns gray and melts, like Alice Through the Looking-Glass.

Housewives never lose touch. Everything they lay their hands on is real, and sometimes nasty, and sometimes terrible, but reality is good for you. Nourishing.

IT CAME ON SUDDENLY. IN THE FALL I WAS SAYING TO people, "Doesn't Boy look good? Isn't he sleek and solid?" When it was almost Christmas, he seemed to be losing weight, and some of his buttery shine. He paid no attention to his Christmas mouse. Even when the house was full of company, instead of stalking outside in a huff, he stayed in, and warmed his ears under a lampshade. Three days after Christmas I took him to the vet.

She found a lump. Probably a tumor, brought on maybe by the years of cystitis to which he had been a patient martyr.

On Monday she checked him again, and said it was growing rapidly. "Keep him as long as he seems comfortable," she said.

I took the remains of a festive leg of lamb from the refrigerator and fed him little shreds of it until he turned his head away.

It was the last day of the year. I sat with him all day, staring out at the rain, and when I spoke to him he looked up, but answering was too hard. There was no reproach or inquiry in his look. He was an intelligent cat, and he seemed to know that the darkness that was stalking him was beyond my powers to fend off.

Sitting there, just waiting, I took down a book on cats from the shelf and began to read, idly. I shouldn't have; I could have had some more days, or weeks even. In the chapter on older cats, the book spoke encouragingly, almost gaily, about malignant tumors and the excellent prospects for their safe removal. It told me stories about cats well on into their twenties, delivered from cancer, waltzing home again to wash their paws and catch flies on their sunny window sills.

I was overcome with hope. Almost certainty. Everything would be all right. Of course it would. Why, ten years was no age for a cat, no age at all, and how could he die, how could he possibly die so soon, and not at twenty or twenty-five, on the foot of my bed, full of crotchets and dignity and long memories?

On the second of January, I gathered him up from where he sat on the sunny side of the house watching wild geese, and rushed him back to the vet. I told her I wanted an immediate operation.

Oh, why didn't she give him a shot? Why pills? We had a wicked struggle getting two Nembutals down him. I am so sorry, my cat. You drooling and pissing with such unbecoming rage and terror. And then the vet offered me gloves to hold you with. *Gloves.* Great horrible padded gloves. As if ever, in any extremity of fear or anger, you would scratch me. I wept, and threw the gloves on the floor, and we went on struggling with the pills, and you thrashed frantically with your eyes dilated, but never laid more than a slim, soft paw on my wrist, begging me to stop.

Then we put him in a cage. (Why couldn't I have taken him out to the car? Why in a cage? *Why,* with the awful smells, and the dogs barking all around, and strangers, and strange cats yelling? You could have fallen asleep on my lap, alone, in the car, and I carried you back in sleeping. Of course, I didn't know it was your last sleep. I was still deranged with hope.)

I sat on the floor beside the cage, and for forty minutes he fought the Nembutal, blind with panic. I was crying, and I had no Kleenex and kept having to use my sleeve, but I still thought I would bring him home. Tomorrow I will go to the grocery store, I thought. I will buy lamb chops, and, bagging my groceries, be sure they're on the top of the bag so I won't have to dig for them. Then I'll drive straight over here. He'll be out of the anesthetic by then, and weak and groggy, but he'll know me, and he'll be too weak to answer but we'll look at each other. I will remember to bring a paring knife, and cut the lamb chops into small easy slivers.

Sleep well, my old man. King of the cats.

And then I went home, mad with hope, and waited for the phone to ring.

It rang. Not a simple tumor, but lymphosarcoma, spreading, inoperable. An unpleasant way to go, with vomiting and diarrhea. Now, if it was *her* cat, and already anesthetized as he was . . .

I told her to go ahead.

And she did.

Driving blind and streaming, I go back to the vet's for the body, and they have wrapped it for me in layers of plastic bag, a strange inhuman bundle. I bring it home, and leave it in the garage for a while, and go inside and cry.

But I have to open it. I can't bury a lump of plastic bags. But I'm afraid. She operated, after all; is he mangled? Horrible?

Shaking hard, I draw out the stiff body.

Not mangled at all. She has curled him up in the position of sleep, with no wound visible, his tail over his folded legs, his eyes shut, his fur sleek and shining. Insane flash of relief: oh, he's *not* dead! Not dead at all.

But he feels cool to the hand.

He looks so like himself. I wrap him lightly in a red towel and lay him on the couch in front of me, and the light from the window makes blue lights in the slick black fur. The point of his long whippy tail is laid on his shoulder, and only his elegant little paws look unnaturally stiff.

He is cold, but the shape of him is so long familiar to my hand. I hope my hand can remember it, at least for a while: the neat slick skull, small shoulder blades, sharp now from losing weight, and the sharp knobs of his spine, and the long thin tail.

He looks good in a red towel. If I spoke to him, would he look up and blink, and spread his toes, and purr?

How can I put him in the ground?

Old man, old man, I must get you ready now. It's a quarter of three, and the children will be home soon, and I don't want them here. I want us to be alone this time, you and me. You would have loved to live alone with me all your life, and you never did, but I will bury you alone. No tears but mine.

I put him on a chair where he used to sleep curled up, and he lay there curled. I stroked and stroked him till my hand was cold. Then a strange thing happened. When I touched him, I heard a sort of purr. Not a real purr, but the breathy soft wheeze of a sleeping cat making a token sleepy thanks for being touched. I knew it couldn't be. I thought it must be my own sleeve rubbing against the towel, or my wheezy chest, or the refrigerator, or the plumbing. I checked everything. Silence. You could hear a feather drop in the house. And I touched my cat again, and there was the breathy rumble, the soft vibration of purr. And again. Over and over. And he was cold, and stiff, but there it was, unmistakable.

In a panic of hope I tried to find a mirror to hold in front of his nose, and could only find an old compact, and tried to use it and got horrid smelly pink powder on his beautiful fur, and gave up.

Dead cats do not purr. I may be distraught but I am scarcely insane. I stopped touching him and pushed it out of my mind.

His little pointy paws were cold, and felt smooth and unworn, as if they should have gone many more miles.

It was a perfect day, raining and freezing so that long tears hung from the rhododendron leaves. I made the hole under the front window, on the south side of the house, where he was sitting watching wild geese when I came to take him away. I lined the hole with the red sweater I had left him with at the vet's. I laid him down, and folded the red towel around him; he always looked splendid in red; and covered his face with the pillow case I had slept on the night before, marked with dry tears and perhaps smelling faintly of me, a last faded scent to take along with him, all I could send.

For ten years he had watched me always with love in his gold eyes. My longest friend. My last lover.

I filled the hole in carefully so as not to get any dirt on his fur, and laid a flat stone over it, and covered it over with branches from our Christmas tree.

Because I am a housewife, and in private life, I can receive this moment of bitter and childish reality with the fullness it deserves.

It rained all night, and then snowed, but the grave is under the eaves and on the south side. Lined with a warm sweater.

His voice is gone, and the silence waits for me in every room. He said a lot of things. Never to complain or demand; he was too proud for that. He was a gentleman, and sat and looked at a door, or a dish, waiting in quiet dignity. He spoke for conversation, and for love, and much of what he said he never said to anyone but me; that he loved me, was glad I had walked into a room, happy to be sitting under a desk lamp watching me work, angry that I was reading when he wanted to be stroked, concerned that I was ill, grateful to be invited to my lap, or to have the door opened. Coming around corners, I can feel myself tensed for his greeting, but it's gone.

Oh, why did we get that damned dog? Soon after she came, she wanted to sleep in our bed. She insisted. Boy fought her off a few times, savagely, but with dumb-dog insensitivity Vicky persisted in sneaking back, and finally, in his dignity and pride, Boy gave up. He would not share. He went downstairs to sleep forever after, unless I was sick and he had to ignore the dog in his concern for me. I should have noticed, and done something, but two people and a dog and a cat are a lot in one bed, and instead of taking note of my old friend's grief, I suppose I was simply glad to have room for my feet.

If I had it to do over, I could put the dog outside. If I had it to do over, I would have no other animals. I always told him he was the senior cat, the premier cat, and he knew it, but it is a long way from being the cat to being merely the senior cat. I could have spoken to him oftener. Sometimes I ignored him, being busy; he never ignored me. I could have patted him without his having to ask. I could have bought kidneys every day.

I see why people believe in ghosts. People need to believe in ghosts. I would love to have the shade of a black cat, sitting on the south side in the winter sunlight. Following me gravely down a path, placing its oval paws precisely in front of each other, and from time to time calling me to wait, because haste is undignified and being carried is humiliating, and he must always follow, at his own deliberate pace.

No other afterlife would please him; I was his whole life and entire love. It would be nice to believe that, buried under the window, in the summertime, when windows are open, he could hear my voice. Not forever, of course, I don't ask the impossible, but just for a little while. Just till we get used to not having each other.

But he'd be so embarrassed by my noisy grief. Look: middle-aged mother of three cries for dead cat.

A person from my old office calls me, bursting with news. Brand & Macomber has gone under, and all the agencies are competing for their accounts. They've made Robin Davies creative director, can I *imagine?* Of course I remember Robin Davies, don't I? Used to free-lance?

Robin Davies? Robin Davies?

"You'd better come in and have lunch with us soon," she says. "It's awful, how you get so completely out of touch with things."

TIME PASSED. WE GOT ANOTHER CAT, AND THROUGH A series of accidents now have four, and the dog, and are fond of them all. Never another black one, though.

Just the other day my husband, rising in what he calls the morning and I call the night, peered out through the dark glass and said, "It's snowing."

I pulled the pillow over my head, unwilling to wake up. "Is Boy out?" I mumbled. He's not in the house. Is he out in the snow?

"*What?*"

"Boy. See if he's at the door."

"You mean Corvo, don't you?"

"Of course." I struggled upward through layers and layers of sleep. "I meant Corvo."

I didn't, though.

Rest well, my old man.

CHAPTER SEVEN

$\mathcal{E}$ mily, on horseback, rode serenely into adoles-
cence, and the boys moved up the numbered rungs
of school, and I realized that it wasn't last year
I'd planted the tomatoes over by the plum tree, but the
year before last. Or maybe the year before that.

The boys' homework enters our life, stormily.

The grunginess of their homework papers rings a depressing bell. The smudges and rips from erasing. The
staggering straggle of long-division problems down a page,
and the acrid smell of trapped, frantic, helpless boredom
rising from it. The battered books that, snatched up in
haste, vomit papers all soft and torn at the edges from
much traveling. Teachers' comments on them. "Messy";
"Finish!"; "You forgot to number problems"; "Underline
verbs"; "B –"; "C +."

I am relieved to be grown up, here and not there.

I am unable to take up a consistent stand on the matter, and veer erratically from "You'll finish it if it takes
you all night" to "You should have thought of it earlier,
it's bedtime now."

My husband finally took over the mathematical areas, after he heard me tell them, in firm authoritative mother-tones, that seven times eight was fifty-four.

He put down the newspaper and slung his legs over the edge of the couch and sat up. "What did you say?"

Insecure, I backed down. "Isn't it?"

"No."

"Well, *something's* fifty-four."

"Six times nine," whispered Matthew apologetically.

"Since you know so much, then, young man," I said, clutching shreds of my authority around me, "why ask me?" I considered claiming I only said that to test them, but abandoned the idea. The truth is I never did learn the multiplication tables except in spots, so that I have to work backward or forward from something I do know, such as seven times seven, which is, I think, forty-nine, only even then I have to hide behind the door to count on my fingers because I have trouble with forty-nine plus seven, too.

My husband, who can figure out in his head how long to cook a five-and-a-half pound chicken at twenty minutes a pound, takes over the math and leaves me the spelling.

I don't know what the more progressive schools do, but in our nostalgic institutions there are still spelling lists to study, and a person has to use each word in a sentence.

I watch over their shoulders. Matthew writes, slowly and messily, "There is one of us, are there one of you?" and I think about that for a while. Indeed, it wakes me up in the middle of the night for several weeks. "There is one of us." Twins. How can it possibly *feel,* to be twins;

closer than love, entangled, no memory of separateness? No wonder they have trouble with singular and plural verbs; no concept of the singular at all.

"What does it mean, 'There is one of us'?" I ask cautiously.

He looks up, baffled, and down at his paper. "It's a sentence. It doesn't mean anything. Just a sentence."

There is one of us.

Sometimes, when I call Ben, Matt answers. I say, "I was calling Ben. You're not Ben," and Matt shrugs, as if the thing were a quibble, and the distinction of no importance.

Benjamin counts on his fingers like me, but his spelling sentences come forth more easily. He writes, "Even happy mice never smile."

Crowds of mice, gravely ecstatic.

"*My* teacher is prettier than Matt's," he says.

"She is not," says Matt.

"She is too. Your teacher's mean. She's old, too. My teacher's only twenty-eight, yours's practically a aquagenarian."

"She is not!"

"Stop arguing and finish your spelling."

My husband says, "I have read this same sentence eleven times. Can't they do their homework somewhere *else?* When *I* was their age . . ."

After a while he goes upstairs to read in bed.

Emily is already upstairs reading in bed.

Arguing, the boys finish their homework, wash parts of their faces, rub toothpaste on the bathroom wall, and go to bed. It is nine thirty-five. A cat yawns, stretches, and resettles itself in the only comfortable chair. The refrigerator is making that buzzing noise again. The light glints off a BB shot on the floor. There are lots of BBs on the floor, though you can't always see them; in case anyone's interested I even know how *many* BBs: one thousand, three hundred. Ben invested several weeks' allowance in them, to have in case he ever gets a BB gun, which he won't, and kept them in an old flashlight. He kept them there until Matt jerked open the flashlight to see why it didn't work. The vacuum cleaner hates them; they're too small and heavy and scuttle away too fast. They've rolled themselves into every corner of the house, even my husband's closet; I think they're alive.

I pick up a book and stare at it for a while and put it back down. I don't feel like reading. I feel tired and itchy.

There's a television program I watch whenever I remember to, but it's on Wednesday and this is only Monday.

I go upstairs and stand awhile in the hall. In our bed, my husband is asleep beside his open book, with a dog on his feet. A line of light shows under Emily's door, and I hear a page turned. Probably *Gone with the Wind* again. She'll be up all night.

It seems undignified to knock and ask her to come back downstairs to read. And certainly there's no place for me to go and sit in her room; even the cats no longer try, and the last time I went to close her windows in a thunderstorm I stepped on a tube of cadmium yellow.

I go back down to the living room, thinking, after

all that's the point, isn't it? To raise your children so independent that at fourteen they have no further need of your society, and much prefer to read alone, with the door shut.

But who is to raise their mothers independent?

What *do* people do in the evenings? What did I used to do? I can't remember.

I could call someone up and chat, but I can't think of anyone I really want to talk to, and besides, they're probably all busy.

Doing what?

I leaf through a magazine, pausing to read every single word of something called "Ten Tasty Cook-ahead Meals." They all sound nasty.

I pick up the local paper from the floor and turn its pages again to see if I missed anything. I didn't. Two new murders in that trailer park outside Coatesville, where they seem to kill each other all the time. Gives them something to do in the evenings, anyway. I read the real estate ads, feeling dimly that things would be better in a different house, but all the ones that sound nice cost several hundred thousand.

Children have punched holes in the black lampshade. They are tiny holes, pinholes, and visible only with the lights on, when they twinkle in little patterns and constellations. I see Orion's belt, one of the few things I can find in the sky, and Polaris. Will my sons grow up to be astronomers, and live on friendly terms with Aldebaran and the Milky Way? Or just be the fellows you call when you need some holes in your lampshade?

A cat turns a somersault in front of the door, his rather dramatic way of saying he wants out, and I let him out. He whisks away into the blackness, a busy night ahead. There will be rows of little fur corpses on the doorstep in the morning.

I make myself a drink. We're out of scotch, so I try rum instead, and it's not bad. I drink it staring into space and feeling sorry for myself.

I wish I was having a marvelous affair with someone. Only I can't think of anyone who'd be both pleasant and practical to have an affair with.

I make myself another drink, and sit down and run consideringly over all the men I know. It occurs to me halfway down the list that no one has asked to have an affair with me in quite some time.

This is a jolt.

I think back to the last party I went to, and how I stood there and stood there, propping up the wall and trying to smile as if I were thinking of something interesting. It was like being thirteen again. Some local band was playing what sounded, to Sinatra-raised ears, like a cat fight in a hailstorm. I didn't know anyone in the room except my hostess, who was busy, and my husband, who had found somebody from his home town and they were off in a corner uproariously reminding each other of people I'd never heard of.

There was a swimming pool outside somewhere, and a lot of girls about Emily's age were drifting around the party in neatly rounded bikinis, their wet hair painted down their backs.

All evening long, not one man came up to introduce himself.

Oh, there was a man around somewhere I'd been talking to, but he went off to fix his drink and never came back.

He hadn't been replaced. Not even by the inevitable drunk who wants to dance, or the inevitable bore who wants to explain the Middle East. In that whole party not one man had evil designs on my person, or so much as wanted to know my name, let alone my phone number.

Am I stuck here, then? Right *here*?

I'm in favor of liberation and independence, but the truth is, I'm not Amelia Earhart or Margaret Mead, and for people like me romantic adventure needs a man. Imagine Dorothy Lamour sitting all by herself on those tropical islands in the moonlight, listening to the small waves of the lagoon lapping the sand. It's just not the same. If she's all by herself, you know perfectly well what she's waiting for.

No man, no adventures.

I gaze sulkily into my rum.

No *different* adventures, anyway. If you're stuck with the man you've already got, then you're stuck with the adventures you're already having. The supermarket, the kids to a lesson, the cat to the vet.

Not that I'd consciously considered anything else, but there had always been the faint, inadmissable possibility that some dazzling man would swoop down out of the blue, or turn up at a party, and take me to Nepal or Leningrad or Corfu, or star me in his next play. Change everything. Give me a chance to be someone else, with a different life.

The thousands of possible lives that used to spread out in front of me have snapped shut into one, and all I get is what I've got. It's time to pass on the possibilities, all those deliciously half-open doors, to my children, and drive them to airports, and wish them bon voyage.

Which would be swell if only I were a nicer person. Less selfish, more gracefully resigned, not so willful and childish.

Maybe they'll take me along, the children. Take me with them when they go to Paris.

Ho. Who goes to Paris with their middle-aged mother? *What* middle-aged mother? Me? Is that *me,* that dowdy housewife-type with the gray in her hair, sitting in that café? Good God.

I make another drink. Now we're almost out of rum, too, and presently there'll be nothing left but that really flaky Bourbon we bring out for the Christmas party.

Bill Emery floats into my mind. Bill Emery, my first lover, in the Virgin Islands, the toad. Still, he's not the only man in the world. I could have an affair, just an ordinary, stay-at-home affair. Everyone does it now. And maybe your middle-aged housewife type doesn't magnetize lecherous strangers at parties, but gee, there must be someone who doesn't care for little girls, someone who'd appreciate the . . . well, the mature, experienced, sophisticated type.

I gaze down at myself, at the sneakers I wear because they've gotten to the really comfortable stage now, and the blue jeans I wear because I bought them for Emily and they were the wrong kind, with the flared bottoms that only doafs wear any more. My sweater came from the dear old thrift shop, back in my city life, and listen, it was a *very good sweater* in its day. Somebody spent a lot of money for that sweater. Once.

Well, if not sophisticated, mature anyway. Think of the French. They're crazy about mature women.

I wonder aimlessly how many housewives are sitting alone in their living rooms at this very minute drinking straight rum and thinking about the French, and how they're crazy about mature women.

The Chinese, for that matter, are crazy about forty-year-old *eggs*.

Still, there must be someone.

Tom? Wally?

Ugh.

According to the statistics, just about everyone in the country is having an affair. Millions and millions and millions of us, all carrying on improper with gents we're not married to.

But how? When? It seems so dreadfully *inconvenient.* Where do they find the time? Do they put on the navy blue dress and announce that they're going to the PTA meeting, remind Emily about her history test and the twins to brush their teeth, and half an hour later they're whooping it up in a motel room spilling champagne on the sheets, the navy blue dress kicked into a corner? In the midst of a passionate embrace, do they suddenly wonder if Matt needs help with his book report, or is Ben watching that terrible program again, and did they remember to put the leftover chicken away or have the cats got it?

And who's at the PTA meeting? Anybody? Nobody but the geriatric kindergarten teacher, tapping her foot and scowling at her watch, and the local motels all packed to the doors and radiating muffled giggles and sighs?

Maybe it would be easier to do it during the day, if my lover could get away from the office. I could revise my schedule to include him:

Vacuum clnr to shop
Call Marge carpool trade Mon.
Emily riding lesson 3:15
Meet lover Holiday Inn 3:45
p.u. boys soccer 4:30
dishwasher sp, flea collars, sandwich meat, bank
call Joan libry meeting

Assuming people can manage all this, squeeze it in somewhere, who, or whom, are they having affairs *with?*

This Bourbon is really poisonous. No wonder the only sober people at our parties are the Bourbon drinkers; they're always the ones that get to drive home.

If I lived in the city again, worked in an office, I might find somebody suitable there. In a little office, you really know everyone too well to sleep with them, and there's not enough choice: too old or too young or too married or too hideous. In a giant corporation, though, I could wander hopefully from department to department, peering and inquiring like Diogenes for a nice man to have an affair with.

But out here in the wilderness the only men I ever see are the neighbors' husbands and the fathers of my children's friends. There's the man who reads the meter, but he's always in a hurry. There's the mailman, but he comes in a car, and it seems a bit gauche to rush out and flag him down and ask if he'd like to come in and have an affair with me.

All right, that leaves David's daddy, and Scott's, and Amy's. Caroline's husband. Ellie's.

I'm not really sure I could manage it. Let's say it's Caroline's husband, though I'm not sure he's much interested in sex; he never talks about anything but money; what do I do? Just walk up to him, assuming I ever see him alone, and say . . . say . . . say what? Hey, Bill, let's have an affair? Or be more subtle? Bat my eyes, touch him on the arm a lot? He wouldn't notice.

Besides, I do have to see all these women, and I'm not a good liar. I tend to sputter and turn a purplish color when uttering even the mildest social fib, like why I can't go to a party. How can I borrow their extension ladder and drink their coffee and carpool their kids if I've been rollicking around in a motel with their husbands half the night?

Maybe total strangers are the answer. But how do you find them, if they never come and speak to you at parties any more?

You could advertise, I suppose. My husband tells me there are publications circulating now that contain nothing but ads for people to do things to people sexually; mostly rather bizarre and strenuous things, I gather, but maybe they accept ads from ordinary housewives looking for ordinary adventures.

But the people who answered your ad, if anyone did, might be horrid. They might even be dangerous. They would very likely be unattractive. Then you'd have to explain that you were really looking for someone nicer, which could lead to harsh feelings.

In more sophisticated areas than this, there are singles bars, so people in search of romance can go find other people in search of romance, which has the advantage of precluding explanations: if you're there, that's what you're there for. The trouble is, it must take time. You can't just rush in and grab up a suitable prospect as if he were a loaf of bread and a dozen eggs. You have to sit with your drink, and look around and get looked at, and go through the is-someone-sitting-here and excuse-me-do-you-have-a-match routines.

You haven't got forever. PTA meetings are usually over by ten, and anyway you have to get up early to make school lunches.

Besides, suppose you sat there all evening with your unlit cigarette and nobody offered to light it for you?

Even if I did score, I think I'd feel horribly shy. Let's face it, I'm pretty much out of date. In *my* day, sex was supposed to be a matter of blind passionate impulse, and now it seems to be kind of serious and technical: tell me what you want me to do to you next, then I'll tell you what to do to me. I'm sure I'd be bad at it, and giggle, or get bored and go home.

I pour the Bourbon down the sink, wondering about the septic tank, and tentatively, with drunken suspicion, try the cooking vermouth. It tastes mean, and thin, and disapproving.

As an alternative to other men, one can try to rekindle romance with one's own. I've been reading a lot about that lately. As I understand it, all you have to do is meet him at the door wearing nothing but high heels and a rose in your teeth, and he snatches you up foaming with passion and drags you off to the bedroom. As a bonus side effect, this gets your children and their little friends to glance up from the television for a minute, which doesn't happen often.

None of the articles say what to do if he doesn't snatch you up foaming. They don't say what the answer is when he says, instead, "What happened? Where are your clothes? Why are you eating that flower? Put something on, you'll freeze." They don't say what to do when he says, "Putting on a little weight, aren't you?" Or, worse, "Boy, am I bushed. What's for dinner?"

They don't say what happens when you bite into the rose, fling open the door, and he's brought Joe Whitaker home with him to talk about the insurance.

I'm all for rekindling romance, I just don't think it's that easy. I think the only way to do it is to put the children in a camp or kennel or something, and fly to London and stay in the best room at the Connaught and have fantastic meals sent up, and go to the theater every night and buy a lot of marvelous clothes.

I lurch over to the cupboard and fumble in it and find my savings bankbook. It contains one hundred and thirteen dollars and forty-three cents.

So much for romance.

So much for adventure.

If I had some more money, I could try having an adventure all by myself. An asexual adventure. Travel or something. Yeah.

Of course I can't set out till after the man comes to look at the refrigerator. *If* he comes. And I have to be back by three-thirty to beat the school bus. That lets out Acapulco and Lapland. I could just about make it to Wilmington, Delaware, and then when I got back there'd still be the laundry to fold, and nothing defrosted for dinner.

Even if I could go to Lapland, I wouldn't enjoy it. I'd feel guilty for not bringing the kids along to pat the baby reindeer.

Clearly, there are a lot of adventures I am simply never going to have. Daydreaming, I have passed all the exits on the expressway; no U-turns. I will never see an elephant that isn't in a zoo, or sail down a fiord, or stand on top of Kilimanjaro or even under it. I will never see a penguin hatchery, or the Parthenon, or even the Eiffel Tower.

Or even Newark.

Besides, since I'm not a pretty girl any more, who would offer to carry my suitcase, or help me if I got lost?

Masochistically I drink the vermouth.

Here I sit in my frayed spotty thrift-shop sweater, all

old and withered and loverless, a housewife and more than a little drunk, and my brains have eroded under the years of small children and breakfast dishes and wiping off the kitchen counter and wiping off the kitchen counter and wiping off the kitchen counter until my mind is furred with mildew like an orange forgotten in the refrigerator, and my husband is asleep, and all the upper corners of the house are draped in cobwebs and the lower corners are dim with dust and dog hairs, and there's a sock and a Magic Marker with no top under the footstool, and nothing left to drink. And this is my *life*. This.

I could take a course in something. Go to classes. Learn something, just to see if I still can, see if this shrunken soggy brain can be stretched back to its former size or if the cells themselves are dead.

Going to night classes is almost as big as adultery around here. Women I know go back for degrees, and advanced degrees, or just to learn about yoga or ceramics or economic theory, or weaving or Great Books or tap dancing or belly dancing or astrology or automobile repairs, or karate or needlepoint or Beginning Spanish or first aid. Even out here in the country there are classes everywhere. Under the hoot of the barn owl and the faraway nickering of a horse you can hear the quiet purposeful hum that means housewives are learning to play the guitar and paint watercolors.

Well, it's an idea, I suppose. It's better than drinking the vermouth. *That* can't be good for the brain cells.

Besides, if you picked your courses carefully, you might even meet a nice man to have an affair with.

ON THE OTHER HAND, IF I MADE EMILY A CUP OF TEA, and called her, maybe she'd come downstairs to drink it.

ON HIS WAY BACK FROM ST. THOMAS, BILL EMERY PHONES again. This time he isn't catching a plane, and has time to come and visit, looking dashing beyond my wildest hopes in whiskers and a big hat. He stays to dinner and spends the night.

In the morning, in return for my hospitality, he most correctly informs me, over breakfast, that he has indeed carried my image like a precious candle flame in his heart through all the years.

This is the kind of thing more people should say to housewives in February.

He mutters sweet nothings into my neck. ". . . as madly in love with you as I ever was."

Gratified, I smirk, and pour more coffee, and call upstairs, "Hey, you guys getting dressed? It's a quarter of!"

He kisses me. I put down the coffeepot and kiss him back.

". . . never forgotten you," he mumbles.

From upstairs: "I don't have any underpants!"

I turn discreetly aside from his embrace without disengaging it, and give my most winsome and ladylike bellow: "Wear some of Ben's, then! But hurry up!"

Bill kisses me again. Ben, on his way to the breakfast table, brushes blindly past our embrace. Ben's life seems to take place somewhere else, in a space warp; he trips over the furniture; the only things he notices don't exist.

He sees things, and walks in his sleep. Probably it's my fault.

"I had three dreams last night," he grumbles, "and they were *all* reruns."

Blushing prettily, I say, "Go and wash your face."

"I already did."

"What's that on your chin, then?"

"That," he says smugly, "isn't dirt. That's an obstacle illusion, that's all."

"Wash it anyway."

From upstairs: "Mom! One of my sneakers is wet!"

Bill Emery gives me a look designed to convey hopeless passion, regret, and devotion, and gets into his car and drives away. Which is fine with me. The man's coming about the pump this morning, and I have to take the posters to the library, and I really don't have time.

However, I feel a great deal better. After the boys get off to school I do a few Stephen Sondheim numbers as I chip the burnt potatoes au gratin off the oven floor.

After all, I console myself, no matter how and with whom, I would still be spending a lot less time on romance and adventure than I spend, for instance, making peanut-butter-and-jelly sandwiches and putting them in Baggies, so it can't be so important as all that.

IN THE CITY, IN AN OFFICE, TIME TENDS TO BE LINEAR, while in the country it is definitely circular. There are moments in, say, March, when you stop and wonder whether that really deep snow was last March, or the March before, or the March before that, and at such moments the calendar, round in the mind like a Mayan calendar, spins so fast it blurs.

JANUARY: Seed catalogues. Great poisonously scarlet tomatoes, pulsing with color, clearly inedible; ugly ladies holding up for the photographer baskets of peaches, baskets of chrysanthemums; ugly men grinning beside pumpkins as big as bulldozers. . . . Snow on the woodpile, snow on the windshield, snow in the boots. The mulish noise of a car that does not intend to start again till April, and indeed, why should it bother, since the driveway is a river of ice down which the children go spinning on scraps of cardboard boxes. . . . Report cards: so-and-so does not pay attention—interrupts—pleasure to have in class—disrespectful—needs to improve study habits—contributes—does not contribute—basic computation skills. . . . The schools close, open, close again. The radio sits on the breakfast table: the following schools will be open an hour late. The following schools will be closed. The following schools will be open without transportation. . . . Gray winter light in the rooms, the color of overcast sky. Evening: slits of red in the seams of the wood stove.

FEBRUARY: Chickadees in the feeder. Titmice, Carolina wrens, Mrs. Cardinal, nuthatches, Mr. Cardinal. Birds moving to and from the feeder are the only things in the landscape that move; the eye is glad for them, and for the red stop sign just visible down the lane, the only color in the white-and-gray. Quiet. The refrigerator motor shuts off; you can hear the cats breathe. Sometimes the far-off snarl of chain saw. Screech of jay. Song sparrows on the ground singing recklessly while they eat. Seed on the snow for sparrows and doves. Snow settles over it; tramp it down, pour out more seed. A layer cake of bird seed and snow from which, in May, this patch will spring up in curious and alien plants. . . . Inside, on the window sill under the feeder, in a wooden bowl lined with a sweater, a cat sleeps with its paws pressed over its face. Even the dimmest cat eventually gives up trying to launch itself through the glass at chickadees. Then, for a whole winter or even two, the cat sits bolt upright on the window sill and watches the feeder with the tip of its tail slashing irritably. Then, finally, the next February, it sleeps, and waits for the mice of spring.

MARCH: Vitamin C. Aspirin. Kleenex. Wads of Kleenex, deep in the pants pockets, go through the wash and come out hard grayish pellets, papier-mâché. We reel from one disease to the next, and I stagger from bedroom to bedroom in the night, the Lady with the Nose Drops: "I *know* you can't breathe. Stop crying, that makes it worse." Noses upturned to receive their Neo-Synephrine. . . . But the sky fills up with geese. The pond melts. Ben brings in sheets of ice, dribbling mud, to put in the freezer against the summer to come; mud trickles down over the packets of frozen beans and freezes there. . . . The ducks are free at last. All winter I have gone out, sometimes three times a day, with a pickax and a kettle of boiling water, to melt them a hole the size of a salad bowl in the ice; they take turns in it. Sometimes they slither and lurch across the snow to the house, and squat on the sill of the sliding doors and peck at the glass. Emily let them in once, and they haven't forgotten. They want to come in and get warm, they want to be lap ducks. In March they forget us. The pond melts and they move in their proper element again, and make love all day.

APRIL: There's no way to dress for April. April is like a treacherous house that's always trying to throw you downstairs or drop plaster in your soup; it keeps turning on you. Season of lost jackets and sweaters, lost raincoats, lost shoes. What you start forth with in the morning turns out to be wrong, and you leave it on the school bus or out by the pond. Sometimes there's a heat wave and I cover the bedroom floor with ancient clothing, looking for bathing suits. . . . The andromeda blooms in long drooping sprays of greeny-white bells and I pick it in reckless abundance, heavy with ice, and heap it in the sink to melt. At least once a year I say, "Where I come from, it's *spring* in April." . . . The mud sucks the boots off your feet. The peas go in, and the lettuce. Peepers call from the dark woods. . . . Emily and I drag the porch furniture out onto the lawn and paint it again.

MAY: Sometimes, in May, if all goes well, you can walk out of the house without doing anything first. Walk out, bootless, coatless, leaving the door open behind you. Walk slowly, with the arms and shoulders loose. Free at last. . . . The grass needs cutting. By the time you've finished the grass in back, the grass in front has grown so tall that a cat, passing on catly errands, shows only a tail and the tips of ears. . . . Peonies bloom, and it rains on them, and they lie down in the mud. The lettuce comes up, but it's not really spring, not yet, not till the corn goes in. All along the roads the fields lie open, waiting for corn, for that secret moment the farmers can feel, like a whisper in their sleep. . . . Twenty-seven more days of school. Twenty-six more days of school. Twenty-five. Twenty-four.

JUNE: *So I shot her on the floor*
          With a loaded forty-four
          And there ain't no teacher any more!

They bring home grocery bags full of paper; they cleaned out their desks. Ben gives me a Mother's Day card and a painting of a Christmas tree with packages under it; Matt gives me a valentine and my suede glove. School is out at noon, they are home at a quarter of one, and eat lunch, and at twenty after two Ben says, "I kind of miss school." "Yeah," says Matt. "Let's go watch television. Nothing else to do." . . . One June (this June? last June?) we went to an orchard to pick cherries. It was cool and sunny and every tree had a million cherries on it and they glowed in the sun like little red lights in the green leaves. Matt and Ben and I picked twenty pounds of cherries. Later, I couldn't figure out what to do with them. Nobody would help me pit them. There were kettles and cartons and saucepans full of them all over the kitchen, an incalculable fortune in rubies. Presently the children had eaten a lot and there were seeds on the floor to step on barefoot.

I still find an occasional cherry seed, under something, wrapped in dust. . . .

JULY: Vicky is afraid of thunderstorms. She hides under our bed, shaking violently. Long chains of thunderstorms rattle the East Coast for weeks. If a cloud covers the sun for a moment, she shakes. If a plane flies over, rumbling, she gives an apologetic glance around the room and sneaks guiltily upstairs, like a tiny withered spinster with a secret vice, to squeeze under the bed. . . . The lettuce has bolted to seed; the tomato stakes I put in so neatly have staggered in thunderstorms and lean dizzily against each other or fall down completely, billowing in tomato vines. . . . The ditches are gaudy with wineberries and we are all sick of picking them. Sick of eating them, sick of sour seedy pies. . . . There are so many people hanging around this house I can't possibly get anything done. I sit on the porch with a book on my lap and stare blindly at the perennial border full of daylilies and feel guilty. I am not working and earning money, nor am I chasing cobwebs and trying to decide what to have for dinner. Well, why should I? I'm *supposed* to just sit sometimes. Remember all those books about moving to the country? I'm supposed to refresh my soul staring at nature; I could even go sit by the stream if it weren't for the mosquitoes, and the nettles. . . . I feel guilty anyway. I can't even read, not in broad *daylight* like that.

AUGUST: If only I could remember to wear shoes when I go down to the garden, I could step on the tomato worms.

But I never remember. I mean, I know they don't *bite* or anything, but if you think I'm going to step on one of those things *barefoot* you're crazy. They're so big. They're so . . . juicy. I squat and pound them to death with a rock, shuddering, and wonder if next year I could just go buy my tomatoes at the grocery store. . . . People give each other zucchini. They bring you zucchini when they come to call, and when they leave you give them your own zucchini to take home. Or to throw discreetly out the car window on the way. Roadsides piled high with discreetly thrown zucchini. . . . The boys set their garter snakes free, and take on a small but angry king snake. It eats hamburger, and fingers. . . . Dewdrop, outgrown, has been replaced (last year? the year before?) by a pretty yellow horse, and Emily and Barby ride at dusk because of the flies by day. They tie their horses to the bumper of the car and come in for a glass of milk and some carrots, and ride away again. It gets dark earlier now; the horses' long-tailed behinds melt off into the evening, down the lane, with a pleasant clopping sound. . . . The arrival of local peaches in the market always catches me by surprise. Soon there will be apples. Soon after that there will be signs along the road saying CIDER. I meet my neighbors in the market, pinching peaches by my side, and we turn to each other and say, as everyone in the temperate zone must say this time of year, "Where did the summer go?"

SEPTEMBER: The first yellow leaf, from a tulip poplar, zigzags down to light on the green grass and strike its familiar terror to the heart: So it's coming back after all, huh? Thousands and thousands of years of seasons have passed over the human animal, and we are never resigned. We always hope that winter was some kind of aberration, a passing climatic phenomenon, and, having survived the last one, we won't be required to go through *that* again. We will, though. . . . I go slowly upstairs and open my closet door and drag out all those grocery bags, loosely fastened with masking tape, and spread their contents on the bedroom floor. Mysteriously, they turn out to be the same things I put in there in May. They haven't improved any. That pink shirt Matthew never wears. I suppose he's outgrown it, but since he never wears it, how can I tell? The same damned sweaters. If the other mitten isn't in here somewhere, why in hell did I save *that* mitten? A Cub Scout shirt, several sizes too small now but stiffly encrusted with hard-earned badges, how can I throw it away? My fingers have barely healed from sewing on badges thick as rhinoceros hide, tougher than armor. Some of Ben's jeans can go to Matthew. Some of Emily's can go to Ben. Remember buy jeans patches. Dentist appt E, 3-ring notebook paper, book covers, dimes from bank milk money, coats from clnr, conf. M's teacher, thermos, haircuts boys Sat. . . . The school bus comes, pauses, leaves; the dogs, pausing only to tip over our garbage cans, go back to their respective homes. Silence . . .

OCTOBER: As I drive around on my errands, or look out the kitchen window, or pick the boys up from soccer, I try to remember to appreciate the autumn leaves. I really do. I say sternly to myself that the dogwoods are particularly red this year, or not so red as last year (unless that was the year before) but I find I can't just keep *looking* at them. My mind drifts. City folk drive hundreds of miles and endure terrible hardship to look at these red and yellow trees, and here I am driving along wondering what to have for dinner. I am becoming country folk. "A primrose by a river's brim / A yellow primrose was to him, / And it was nothing more." Me too. Wordsworth was city folk at heart. . . . The hunt goes down the lane, and half a dozen foxhounds, always fascinated by our property as by no one else's, detach themselves and swarm over the lawn and chase the ducks into the pond. A woman draws a pistol and leaps off her horse, throwing the reins to a friend, and races across the yard firing blanks into the air and apologizing to me. The foxhounds, abashed, go back to their pack. . . . "Are you sure you don't have any homework?" "Emily, you'd better turn that light out and go to sleep, it's past eleven." "I can't find my other sneaker, and it's gym today." "Not baloney and cheese *again?*" "Mom, you haven't done anything about my Halloween costume and it's *Thursday* already."

NOVEMBER: Was it the winter before last we got the wood stove? Or before that? I can't remember not having it. I am addicted to it; I will *not* turn on the heat, I won't. I rise dizzily from sickbed to haul its logs. I crouch in front of it early in the morning coaxing it with flattery and newspapers, surrounded by impatient cats. The little Burmese sometimes jumps inside while I'm trying to encourage a flame, and gets all ashy. A really smart cat will

ignore my fussing at the stove door and leap onto the
mantelpiece by the stovepipe, where delicate quivers of
heat can be felt long before the stove warms up. My sons
lurk upstairs in bed for ten minutes after my first audible
thumps and rattlings before they skitter down dribbling
socks and shirts to dress by the stovepipe. We are all
pleased by the ritual, and secretly pretend we don't have
excellent electric baseboard heat. We pretend we would
freeze to death if the stove went out. . . . Whenever someone opens a door, leaves blow in. There are leaves everywhere. Under the dining room table. I don't know whether
to sweep or rake. . . . The whole family is back in one
room again, the warm room. Matt says, "What does e-x-
c-i-t-e-m-e—" "Excitement," I say. "What does—" "Shut
up," says Emily. Ben says, "Listen. Hey, listen. Listen to
this. 'One day Tom was in the act of dosing the crack
when his aunt's yellow cat came along, purring, eying
the teaspoon'—what does a-v-a-r-i-c—" Emily says, "Oh,
shut *up*," and tries to hold her ears, but you can't turn
pages with your fingers in your ears. My husband says,
"There's a recipe in the *Times* for curried eggplant," and
all the children gag. I say, "Are you sure you don't have
any homework?" and Ben says, "I had some math, but
I left my math book on the bus," and Emily stamps upstairs to her icy room to read under the covers. Presently
my husband goes up too, and then the boys, quarreling
aimlessly over which toothbrush is whose. . . . I sit for a
long time and look at the black wood stove as if it was
an open fire. . . .

DECEMBER: I make lists, and clean the house for the Christmas party. Annually I think, If I never invited anyone taller than I am, it would save a hell of a lot of work. However, this would leave out several very old and dear friends, so for their sake I stand on a chair and wipe off the top of the refrigerator and freezer, and run a sponge along the tops of the curtain rods, and the upper edges of the window frames, and swab down the top shelves in the cupboards just in case, in the middle of the party, John Moran might want the cornstarch, or that candied ginger I bought and never used. . . . I take everything off the wooden furniture and wipe it down with lemon oil. . . . I kneel under the sink and root among the filthy cleaning rags and cans of shoe polish and all those half empty box es of Ajax, and am rewarded with an elderly eggshell. . . . I dust light bulbs, and fall off a chair. . . . I take all those drawers and complicated doodads out of the refrigerator and wash it with baking soda, and the next day someone spills a quart of orange juice in it. . . . I polish the silver, and the brass, and the copper, and by this time the laundry is piled up eye-high and everyone's sick of hot dogs and beans for dinner and the cobwebs I swept down last week are back again. The day before the party I mop and vacuum everything that doesn't run faster than I do, and explain in most unmaternal tones what will happen to people who don't take their boots off outside. . . . The party passes in a daze of exhaustion. . . . The Cub Scouts squeeze into their shirts and go to spread cheer singing carols in the old folks' home. Ben reports, outraged, that two old ladies turned their hearing aids off. . . .

Christmas. . . . Was it last year we bought the new lights for the tree? Or was that the year we had all the snow, or the year Emily got her guitar, or was it the year of the electric trains, or the year Mom knocked the tree over, or the year that Boy got sick? (Shadow of a black cat across the heart, like something dim but ominous in an X-ray. Outside the window there, where I put him. Come home, please come home; it's so cold out there and we'll have snow before night. Come in and get warm by the stove.) Was it the second year we were here, or the third, or the year the pond was already frozen by Christmas, or the year we had to go clear to Yellow Springs Road for a tree, and it was so prickly that nobody helped me trim it? The wheel spins faster all the time and the Christmases blur. . . . I can see and smell the fire that sucked all the Christmas cards down off the mantel. That was the boys' first Christmas. . . . I can see Emily's first Christmas, Emily's first stocking, in the apartment where we lived so cozily together, eating chicken noodle soup. . . . I make myself quite a stiff drink before lunch.

JANUARY: Seed catalogues . . .

THE FUTURE PRESSES ON US ALL.

Ben says, "When I grow up, I'm going to be a scientist."

I turn off the vacuum cleaner and sit down. "That's fine. Now, first you have to think about all the different kinds of scientists there are. There's natural science, like biology, where you study—"

He waves me aside. "Not *that* kind. Not like that. I'm going to be a *mad* scientist."

ANOTHER DAY HE COMES TO ME BROODILY; HE HAS changed his mind. He is going to be the person who catches all, all, all the frogs in the whole world, and keeps them safe in a big pond, or a lake maybe, and watches over them. He will bind up their wounds and nurse them in sickness, and feed them flies from his own hands.

My son the Frog Fairy.

Matt is more practical; he worries about how much money he will make, because he plans to marry and have two children. Ben sulks, jealous. If Matt marries, he says, then he will come and move in and live with Matt and his wife, and Matt's wife can cook and clean up for them both, because somebody has to cook and clean up.

CHAPTER EIGHT

*C*hildren let go of your hand, and go over to stand with their own generation.

Emily is in love. She blooms and wilts and blooms again at the whim of some horrible stranger.

She cleans up her room and throws away the collection of old shoes and the many little plastic horses. Certain dear books (*Little Women, Bambi, Anne of Green Gables*) she packs in a carton and puts away in the back of her closet.

The horrible stranger darkens my doorways. He is enormously embarrassed but dead game, and we stare at each other astonished, as if neither of us had expected to meet anyone around this particular corner.

Corner; good heavens, I never even noticed there was a *door* there, and it's another whole room, another country, on the other side. The passage of time, always subject to curious lurches, makes one, and Emily, no longer free and singing, takes her first step toward the bubble gum on the bathroom rug. The moment when there isn't any laundry but my own comes into sharper focus. What an

odd journey this is, jerked forward by other people's jour-
neys. I pause to be pleased by the mad scientist and the
great frog pond, and by Matt still comfortable as a cat in
the branches of the tallest trees. The same branches where
(two years ago? three?) Emily used to rock and sing.

The horrible stranger offers me, tentatively, a smile
with braces in it that would melt a rock, and I go to set
another place at the table.

Some time later, in a dark corner of the pantry, I
stumble over Emily's hard hat. There is an onion in it,
rotting.

BENJAMIN SAYS, "JIMMY SAYS IT'S A COPPERHEAD AND WE
have to kill it."

I say, "Look, stupid, it's not a copperhead. Use your
eyes. It's a milk snake, here's the picture right here. Read
what it says: 'Dark red blotches with black borders on a
cream-colored background.' Isn't that what it's got?"

"Jimmy says you ought to kill them anyway, even if
you aren't sure it's a copperhead. Just in case."

"Yeah, and Jimmy told you if a dragonfly stings you
just once you die. We are not only not sure it's a copperhead, we are positive it's a milk snake. You just go turn
it loose in the woods right now. Somewhere where Jimmy
can't find it."

"Jimmy says his dad always kills snakes. He says you
never know."

I control myself on the subject of Jimmy's dad. The
milk snake is lovely with a stylized elegance that makes
me think of Istanbul, which secretly I call Constantinople,

and is patiently trying to understand being in the bottom of a coffee can. "I'm ashamed of you, you've always been a friend to snakes. Remember Louise? Why would you listen to *Jimmy?* Now take it and turn it loose, *gently,* and you can tell Jimmy from me that if he kills any snake on our property" (we country folk say "property" a lot) "*any* snake, no matter how sure he is it's a copperhead, because I don't think Jimmy knows a copperhead from a dragonfly, then I'm going to spank him and I don't care if he *is* twelve. Do you hear me? Tell him *your mother said so.*"

I fix him with the maternal eye, and realize unsettlingly that very soon now the maternal eye and his will be on the same level.

"Jimmy doesn't know everything," says Matt loyally.

"Yeah," says Ben. "He thinks a crayfish can cut your finger off."

"Copperhead," says Matt. "Huh. What does *he* know?"

They go away with the coffee can, toward the woods. I have won. But not for long.

I can feel myself receding into the distance. Getting smaller. My first child can hardly see me at all any more. She is no longer affected by our local weather, and lives in that state where the rest of the world bleaches out, loses all color and distinction in a whitish blur, and any voice from outside is an interruption to the awful concentration of love.

Sometimes Matt and Ben can still see me, but I have to plant myself in their path, and shout.

It occurs to me that the boys have not been to the dentist in a disreputably long time.

After the first child, there are lots of things you stop worrying about, like whether their teeth are rotting, and their language; Emily wasn't allowed even an occasional "damn," but the twins' language would color the cheek of a drunken stevedore. Not my cheek, though. I pretend not to hear. For one thing, there are always some people standing around at the time, and if I tell the boys not to say it, I will have to explain why not, and what it really means, and some of what it really means is pretty complicated and would require diagrams, and anyway once they found out what it meant they'd find it absolutely delightful and say it all the time. So I stare off into the distance and smile deafly.

About once a year I pull myself together and worry about their evil language, their social adjustment, their schoolwork, and their teeth.

I am so grievously lax about dentists that I haven't bothered to find one out here, so I make another appointment with the one in town. We will drive in. We'll make a day of it this time; have lunch, and visit my old office, and go see the house the boys have forgotten, where we used to live.

The three of us rummage in our closets. The boys have only sneakers, and Ben's are wet and have to be put in the oven. I have sneakers, and a pair of black pumps with high heels and gold buckles, and a pair of loafers all come apart at the seams and fit only for stomping tomato worms. I select the sneakers. At least my jeans are clean.

We drive down the lane and turn onto the back road, and from there to another back road, getting stuck behind tractors and prehistoric pickup trucks, and from there to Route 29, and from there to the expressway. The pickup trucks are replaced by great big trucks with, the boys tell me, eighteen wheels, that roar past like the end of the world and suck our little car whirling along behind them.

It suddenly occurs to me that I should have cleaned out the car. Suppose we're in a wreck? Suppose we have to be pushed, or towed, or it has one of its fits and won't start, and some man comes and slides into the driver's seat and says, "Here, *I'll* start it for you"? He won't, of course, be able to start it any more than I can, but think of the mess of used Kleenex and Wash-n-Dris and empty cigarette packs and cash-register slips and somebody's bathing suit and somebody's ice skates, and the way it smells like a corpse.

The traffic and the air thicken. In the seat behind me the boys go tense. Cars cut in front of us, and make death-defying merges, refusing to yield. Nobody ever yields to this car; it's that kind of car. Ben scrunches down on the floor of the back seat.

"I should have brought my blanket," says Matt.

Ben's voice, from the filthy depths: "I can't look. We're speeding toward inedible disaster."

"Don't be silly," I say, my knuckles white on the wheel. "People drive to town every day. Dad drives to town."

The skyline rises up from the smog, and Ben rises from the floor to admire it, with leaves and bits of candy wrappers in his hair.

We go up a ramp and are suddenly in the city.

"What's happening?" says Matt.

"What do you mean, what's happening?" I mumble, trying to remember which streets are one way which way.

"Why are there all those people?"

"There are always all those people. Nothing's happening."

Ben says, "Do any of those buildings ever, like, just . . . fall *down?*"

"No. Shut up, don't talk to me."

There was a time, long ago, when I searched ardently for parking places in the streets, and worried my way into them like a terrier into a rat hole, blocking traffic, horns blowing, cabbies cursing. I have lost my nerve. I head for a parking garage, one of those great hollow honeycombs smelling of cement, with a sub-subbasement level and a long spiral of ramp that goes up and up, level C, level D; Kafka would have loved it.

We corkscrew upward.

"No," says Ben. "*No.* Please."

"How can we get *out?*" says Matt.

"It's all right," I say cheerfully. "Everything's all right. Don't worry, everything's all . . ." We find a place, high up, and take an elevator back down. The boys don't like the elevator either. I have already forgotten what level we're on, and will never see my little car again.

We walk through the hot streets. I try to look like a native, eyes straight ahead, and wish I could swing my arms with the easy assurance of those who live here, but I can't with a boy fastened to each hand. If they lose their grips, even for the flick of a second, they will instantly be hopelessly and forever lost, and eaten by a bus. Buildings will fall on them.

The dentist finds a small cavity in Ben, and none in Matt, who lives on white sugar and forbidden gum. They do not brush their teeth unless I stand over them with the ruler, which I mostly don't. I am disappointed in the dentist; make a liar out of me, will you? It's time to look for a dentist at home, a dentist who will find all the cavities I have promised my sons.

We walk to my old office. The boys don't remember it.

"You used to come here often."

"We did?"

They have forgotten the elevator buttons, the inter-office phones, the water cooler, the time they broke the adding machine. Awed and skeptical, they consider the urban life of these sophisticated creatures I claim were they.

There's a new girl at the front desk; she seems quite dismayed to see us. The bosses greet us, and my old cronies, or anyway some of my old cronies, who introduce me to the new people, and there is general remarking that the twins have grown in the last six years.

The old art director is still there, and grandly offers them the use of the duplicating machine if they'd like to draw a picture. They back away. I show them my old desk chair, and tell them they used to spin each other in it, and may now if they like. They shake their heads, and draw closer together.

"Well," says an old crony. "So. How are things in the country?"

"Fine. Cooler than here."

"I suppose you're still growing tomatoes, and all that sort of thing?"

"Yes. Well! I see you still have the Whitby account."

"Yes. We still have it. We keep trying to lose it, but it won't leave."

I smile. There is nothing to say. I don't live here any more. I don't have a public face to wear, or public things to say; I don't even have any public shoes. A procession of shoes I used to own appears to me. There was one pair specially, in yellow satin, with pointy toes. Boy, *that* was a long time ago.

The boys and I take a ceremonial drink from the water cooler and leave. No one says to come again.

Lunch, anyway, is a great success, since it isn't Gino's. It's a crummy little place smelling of greasy soup and seems to have gotten even nastier than it used to be, but the boys are impressed by a menu, and a waitress. They change their minds five or six times, and try to engage the waitress in banter, but she's busy.

We head for our old home, in our old alley. "It's too hot," Matt whines. "How far is it? Can't we just go home? Our real home, I mean."

But Ben wants to see where we used to live and so do I.

There are pigeons in the park. There always were. Pigeons, and little boys to chase them, arms outspread, until the whole flock peels away from the ground and curves off flapping like a bedsheet beyond the empty concrete fountain and settles again on the littered grass.

"Look, *birds*."

"Yeah. Birds in the *city?*"

"Pigeons," I say. "They're city birds. You used to chase them, when you were about the size of that little boy chasing them now."

"We did?"

"Hey." Noisy whisper. "What's the matter with that man over there? Is he *drunk?*"

"Probably."

They are mightily impressed. The bum nods and snores on his bench.

We walk, and it's farther than it used to be. My feet have forgotten concrete.

"Well, boys, this is it."

We stand at the mouth of our alley and look down its length. The old wooden fence that used to sag out over the sidewalk, wallowing in vines, has been replaced by something neater in concrete block, and the vines are gone. The Cat Lady's little alley, crossing ours, has changed completely; its whole row of tiny brick houses has been scrubbed and shored up straight somehow, and the doors and window frames replaced and painted Chinese red, and it looks very chic and expensive. Only, what happened to the Cat Lady? Relocated to some high-rise low-income project? What about the cats? How many was she allowed to take with her? Any at all? Betsey's mother, who was always her special companion? Or not?

The two gingko trees I used to take such care of, and

carry water to in July, have survived and prospered, and the little maple, the one delivery trucks kept chopping pieces out of, has grown till it shades the whole end of the alley.

"That's our house," I tell the boys. "The second one from the corner."

It hasn't changed at all. They've even painted the door the same color we always painted it, chocolate brown.

"They all look alike," says Ben critically.

"No, they don't. The doors are different colors."

We gaze respectfully at our old home, and I point out the boys' bedroom windows. Ben remembers, or pretends to remember, the kitchen and part of the front hall, though he isn't sure about the latter. I wonder if the fireplace ever fell into the dining room.

Matt wants to go home.

We GO HOME. WITH SOME DIFFICULTY AND GREAT danger I take off my sneakers in the car and drive barefoot. The city drops away behind us. After a while the air gets cooler.

At home, the boys head for the pond, and I go to stare dismally into the freezer, wondering what to have for dinner and whether, just once, magically, we could have no dinner at all and no one would notice.

It is too late to thaw the chicken. I look on the shelves. Black bean soup. The boys hate it. Canned spaghetti sauce. Stir in the bean sprouts. Taste-tempting variations; sprinkle the top with Cat Chows, run it under the broiler. Rice, noodles, macaroni. Nutmeg. Cheerios, but the box is empty. A jelly glass containing two petrified paint-brushes and still smelling faintly of turpentine.

Like Scarlett O'Hara, I decide to worry about it later, and go to pick up last night's newspaper and stack it, and toss a handful of Legos toward the stairs, to be carried up someday. Wondering dimly about socks, I reach into the open drier, and scream and jump back. This happens all the time, but somehow I never get used to it; there's something about reaching into a dark drier and touching that warm living body in there that's hard to get used to. The cat, stretching and complaining, emerges from the drier and asks about dinner. I feed it, and the other cats and the dog, grateful to them for eating the same automatic food every day. Putting their dishes down I notice how dirty the kitchen floor is. Tomorrow I must mop it. Somebody must. Somebody is me.

We are out of laundry soap, Band-Aids, orange juice, mayonnaise, and Cheerios.

The world has contracted into this small space, and I live in the space, now fully seizin of my housewifehood, a person of private use and function only.

It has its moments. I remember moments in this private life, short ones, of terrific beauty. I remember Emily and her boy friend capering barefoot on the lawn in the green light of an approaching thunderstorm. The green is so very queer and dark that all over the garden lightning bugs appear, lighting up suddenly in the afternoon. Emily flings herself down in the grass with her face turned up to the dark sky, and her boy friend, in the doorway with his silver smile, calls her in from the storm as if she were a cat. She puts her hands behind her head and laughs up at the sky.

Yes, but. Yes, but if they are only moments, what use are they? What good are they if they don't go on forever, and be the whole substance of life? What use is half a handful of pictures?

I don't know. They must *stay* somewhere, somewhere where they do go on forever, with the light always dark green like that, and the afternoon lightning bugs, and Emily always there in the grass laughing. They must pack down somewhere in the subsoil of the mind, or hang somewhere loose in the air, and stay. But whether they stay or fade off into nothing, maybe they're all there is.

Maybe, hell. They are. The rest is just bread crumbs. Filler. Padding.

Matt and Ben come banging into the pantry, tracking mud, carrying a Mason jar full of very dirty water.

"Take that back outside," I say automatically.

"No, wait. Look. I caught a crayfish, look!"

They set the jar on the kitchen table, and we gather around it. "I don't see any crayfish," I complain.

Ben shakes the jar and the mud swirls. "I *thought* I caught a crayfish. He was right *there*. I know I got him. He's got to be in there. Somewhere."

"Maybe he's down in the mud," says Matt. "In the bottom. He was pretty little."

We stare hard into the settling mud. Perhaps he's in there, perhaps not. Other things are in there, things so tiny as to have no form at all to the naked eye, just motion. They seem to swirl aimlessly among the particles of mud, but I suppose they must have purposes of their own. Infinitely tiny purposes, making no impact on the great world.

"I think I saw something move," says Matt. "Down in the mud."

"That's him, then," says Ben, excited, and shakes the water up again. "Where'd you see him?"

I have dinner still to think about, and I never made the beds this morning, but I stand there for a long time anyway, watching the small world in the Mason jar. It's quite remarkable, in its way.

AN AFTERWORD

*R*ereading *In Private Life* for the preparation of this COMMON READER EDITION, I was stunned by how much has changed in such a small handful of years.

I suppose some aspects of private life never change, and probably the children of the turn of the century have much in common with the children of the late 1970s, but in some ways I might have written the *Dead Sea Scrolls*.

On the one hand, there was nothing quaint or virtuous then about a family sitting down to a home-cooked dinner together every night and then reading till bedtime. There was nothing noteworthy about kids who went outdoors unsupervised to build treehouses, catch frogs, and get dirty and wet.

On the other hand, there was nothing sinister then about a mother—a *mother*—who smoked cigarettes, belted down a couple of snorts before dinner, and even invited friends over to abuse alcohol. There was nothing peculiar about a father who largely ignored his children; the paternal role was still limited to its age-old functions of math homework and punishments.

Currently, a married woman who considers having an affair is the vilest of creatures, but sex was a sunnier matter then. Sex in the 70s was like exercise in the 90s, essential for physical and spiritual vigor, and an extra-marital roll in the hay could be a creative alternative to divorce.

Domestic virtues and vices have shifted focus. The endless nightmare of what to make for dinner, haunting women—or at least women prosperous enough to have a choice—throughout their history, has vanished with-out a trace. Our world allowed us to drink and smoke, even in the presence of our young, but it never let us dodge dinner. Take-out or carry-home food was strictly for bachelors, and a frozen dinner, prepared by the hands of strangers, was reserved for times of crisis and regard-ed by the children as a rare treat and by the adults as a shiftless abdication of responsibility. Taking the whole group out to McDonald's positively glittered with sinful-ness; most families indulged only for birthdays.

Dinner was the linchpin of domestic life. Automatical-ly, without prearrangement, the family assembled, hands were washed, the table was set by the designated child, and people ate what was put in front of them, not always uncomplainingly but always without alternatives, and con-versed on topics of general interest, like "He's kicking me under the table" and "You know I hate tunafish."

An ancient custom, gone in the blink of an eye. An incalculable load lifted from the domestic shoulders.

The rest of the private load—vacuuming, scrubbing, picking bubblegum out of the bathroom rug—has faded, if not from actual life, at least from public dialogue. Apparently it's no longer a problem. I don't know how people manage, but manage they must. Maybe they just dash out at lunchtime and buy a new bathroom rug, or a whole new house.

Parents now rear their children more solemnly, perhaps because they have fewer of them and waited longer for their arrival. They can't seem to take them for granted, and this detracts from their entertainment value. Even in my most sleep-deprived triple-career days, mothering from seven till nine, working from nine till five, cooking and mothering from five till nine, and writing from nine till one, a houseful of kids always felt like terrific fun. It added texture and variety to life, and laughs, and good stories to tell, and a kind of sensuous, physical reality to the world. If I had it to do over again, I'd have more.

At our house back in the city, no children play now in the alley where Emily learned to ride a two-wheeler; the children have moved indoors. At the house where we lived in the country, with its rickety pen for the pony and its pond full of frogs, housing developments and shopping malls now stretch away to the horizons.

Funny, it seems only yesterday.

And strangely enough, it was.

Barbara Holland
Bluemont, Virginia 1996

Barbara Holland has lived in a variety of worlds. *In Private Life* is the chronicle of her years as a mother, first urban and gainfully employed, then rural and thrust full-time into a maelstrom of children and other dependents. Currently she lives in the Blue Ridge mountains of Virginia with several cats and an occasional bear or mountain lion.